POVERTY SUCKS!

How to Become a Self-Made Millionaire

Aimee Elizabeth

If you purchase this book without a cover, you should be aware that this book may have been stolen property and reported as "unsold and destroyed" to the publisher. In such case, neither the author nor the publisher has received any payment for this "stripped book."

This publication is designed to provide competent and reliable information regarding the subject matter covered. However, it is sold with the understanding that the author and publisher are not engaged in rendering legal, financial, or other professional advice. Laws and practices often vary from state to state and if legal or other expert assistance is required, the services of a professional should be sought. The author and publisher specifically disclaim any liability that is incurred from the use or application of the contents of this book.

Copyright registered 2011 by Aimee Elizabeth and Michael Forrest Murray.
All rights reserved.

Published by: MFM Trust, 1681 Parkchester Drive, Las Vegas, NV 89108.

Printed in the United States of America.

First Printing: November, 2011.

ISBN: 978-0-9847699-9-5

Library of Congress Control Number: 2011942025

Website Designed by: MM Consulting International, www.mmci.ws

To Learn More about our e-business consulting, Visit Our Website at: **www.AimeeElizabeth.net**

This book is dedicated to everyone who agrees that

POVERTY SUCKS!

You deserve a better life.

Start now.

I Have a Dream!

How wonderful would it be for everyone who is physically able to work to read my book and then be equipped with the knowledge and training to be able to get off of welfare and unemployment lines, regain their dignity, and need no more government handouts?

How wonderful would that be for the taxpayers?

How even more wonderful for the government officials who were smart enough to promote my simple five-point wealth building plan?

Those government officials would become *true heroes* of our nation – saving the taxpayers *billions* of dollars and helping to balance the federal budget! And they wouldn't be kicking anyone off of the entitlement programs in the meantime while people are learning.

This book could change the lives of everyone who reads it. It could change our entire nation – and all for the better!

This is my dream. I hope you *and* our politicians will help to make it come true.

-Aimee Elizabeth

ACKNOWLEDGEMENTS:

Due to legal and privacy reasons, I will need to leave most of my thanks anonymous. All of the names of the people mentioned in this book have been changed to protect the privacy of those involved.

There are so many people I want to thank, for the love, support and kindness they showed me when my life was so difficult in high school. I will never forget all that you did for me and all that you will always mean to me.

I want to thank all my loved ones, who always believe in me, always love me, and whose unwavering love and support always helps to give me the strength to reach my dreams. You all know who you are, and I thank you for being in my life and for giving it meaning and value.

Special thanks to Dixie, who nicknamed me "Miss Contingency Plan."

Special thanks to Mike and Martha, for all that you will always mean to me.

Special thanks to Dena Dunkelberger, for being the absolute best employee and best manager I ever had in all my years of business ownership.

And thanks to everyone who reads my book. I wish you great success in your quest for financial security and an early retirement!

To Learn More about our e-business consulting:

Visit our website at:
www.AimeeElizabeth.net

TABLE OF CONTENTS

CHAPTER ONE.......1
Who the Heck Am I and Why Should You Take Advice from *Me*?

An overview of my life and the adversity I faced. How I bucked the system and went from *my* rags to riches, and how I'm going to teach *you* to do so, too!

CHAPTER TWO........11
***I'll Try, I Can't* and Other Things Losers Love to Say**

A definition of losers. Learning to trust in *you*. Overcoming fear. Important business traps to be avoided. Lessons learned. Business Criteria - My "Rule of Five."

CHAPTER THREE.......17
I Will, *I Can* and Other Things Winners Have to Say

Why the commitment of *I Will* and *I Can* are the keys to business success. Learning to stay focused. The power of being Eternally Optimistic. Persistence pays off!

CHAPTER FOUR.......21
How to Decide Which Business is Right for You

Six questions that will change your life. Residual income. Running your business from home. Interviewing the competition. Replace yourself. Unexpected surprises. Picking a winner!

CHAPTER FIVE.......27
Brainstorm Your Way to Success
How to take fun hobbies and turn them into your dream business. Not every business is a winner – and how to tell the difference! Lists, bookstores, classes and the internet.

CHAPTER SIX.......33
Do What You Love

Selecting the business that's right for you. If you had a million dollars…what would *you* do? 18 sample businesses that fit my "Rule of Five" criteria. Time to do your due diligence!

CHAPTER SEVEN.......39
What to Do If You *Still* Can't Find the Right Business for You

Professional help – *free of charge!* Dos and don'ts. How to handle garbarge fees. No exclusivity! SBA Loans. Training Period. Invoicing Your Clients. Operating Expenses. Alternate financing. NDAs.

CHAPTER EIGHT.......53
Running the Numbers

How to keep your start up costs low. Selecting your business entity. CPAs, business licenses, bonding and liability insurance. Advertising and marketing costs. Plan for the worst and shoot for the best.

CHAPTER NINE.......65
The Importance of Details

Preparing a step-by-step startup checklist. Funding your new business. How to find an honest attorney - honestly! How to advertise, market and promote easily and successfully. Go above and beyond the call of duty.

CHAPTER TEN.......77
Banking On a Winner

Selecting the right bank for your new business. Online vs. physical banking. Large national banks vs. small community banks. Freebies! To borrow or not to borrow? Maintaining financial diligence.

CHAPTER ELEVEN.......83
Work Smart, Not Hard

How to grow your new business. How to close a deal. Make a Friend, Make a Sale! Handling problems easily. When and how to hire and treat outside help. Non-compete agreements.

CHAPTER TWELVE.......101
I Quit! **How to Know When the Time is Right**

Knowing when to quit your day job. Maintaining health insurance. Some pitfalls to avoid. Making the split easier. Who to tell what and why. Breaking the "employee" mentality.

CHAPTER THIRTEEN.......113
Finding Your First Rental Property

How to select your first rental property. HOAs – yes or no? What an agent will do and how to find the right one. Depreciation and taxes. Ready-made rental units: good or bad? Handling buyer's remorse.

CHAPTER FOURTEEN.......133
The Importance of Homeowners Insurance

Choosing a personal insurance agent vs. a commercial insurance broker. Insurance deductibles – how high? Lawsuits and how to avoid them. Why you need an umbrella liability policy.

CHAPTER FIFTEEN.......141
Funding Your First Rental Property

Finding the right mortgage broker. How to contract for success! Protect yourself at close of escrow. Interest rates and loan terms. How to tell a good loan from a bad loan. Finding the best funding. Fannie Mae deals.

CHAPTER SIXTEEN.......157
Finding and Keeping Reliable Tenants

How much to charge for rent? How to find your tenants. Referrals. Welfare tenants. No discrimination! Pets? Finding a good (and free!) rental contract. How to collect the rent. How to handle evictions and still love what you do.

CHAPTER SEVENTEEN.......175
How to Choose and Train a Manager for Your Service Business

Hire a manager or sell your business? Promote from within or hire an outsider? How to select your manager. Training your new manager. Payment and motivation.

CHAPTER EIGHTEEN.......185
How and When to Sell Your Service Business

How to decide when it's time to sell. How to find a reputable business broker. Getting a free business evaluation. Setting your "asking price." Finding a buyer for your business. Negotiating the best deal.

CHAPTER NINETEEN.......195
Your Five *Easy* Steps to Wealth and Early Retirement

How to retire early. Live low, save high! Diversifying your investments. CDs, tax free munis, annuities, life insurance, mutual funds and dollar-cost-averaging. Financial advisors. K.I.S.S. and tell! My Five Point Plan.

CHAPTER ONE

Who the Heck Am I and
Why Should You Take Advice from *Me?*

You don't know me, and that's a shame. Because if you did, you might well be independently wealthy by now. I could have shown you how to make yourself a fortune, and you could have done so long ago.

Me? How could I have shown you the road to riches and financial independence?

How could I have missed? After all, my wealth building credentials are impeccable. I was kicked out of the house when I was 15, left to my own devices. I could have died from disease or wound up in jail or on drugs. I barely managed to finish high school.

Yet, at the age of 38, I retired well on my way to becoming a multi-millionaire.

At the age of 47, I decided to share my formula for success with the world.

But I'm getting ahead of myself. Let me go back.

I was raised in the best of families and the worst of families. My adopted father loved me like crazy when it was convenient, and my mother told me she never wanted to adopt me at all.

Dad and all of my teachers used to tell me that I could do anything I wanted in life, and I believed them. Mom disparaged my independence since she was from one of the last generations of moms who didn't work. Like most dysfunctional families, it functioned, sort of, for many years. I remember feeling happy enough at the time. I knew nothing else. And then my father found a new pastime.

Her name was Peggy or Katie or Sue - it didn't really matter - and she was his secretary. When dad's affair became so blatant that he came home only late Saturday nights and left again early Sunday mornings (allegedly for work), mom's drinking went totally off the rails. And the walls came tumbling down on the house of lies they had built around themselves. And me.

Rather than face her failing marriage, my mother set out to make me the scapegoat, probably in a desperate attempt to regain the attention of her cheating husband. I'll never truly understand their motivations, but the bottom line is that I went virtually overnight from being the family favorite, a great student, and all-around good kid, to being Public Enemy Number One - at least in the eyes of my mother. I begged my father to help me. But he was too busy entertaining his 18-year-old girlfriend to be bothered. Besides, risking my mother's wrath by standing up to her might have caused him to miss out on a little action with his new girl. Heaven forbid.

Things took a sudden turn for the worse when my mother, who had waited until dad was out of town, decided to lock me out of the house. I was 15 at the time, a sophomore in high school, and I couldn't use my key to open the front door, as the screen door was locked. Perplexed, I rang the doorbell. When she answered, my mother told me to take all my clothes because I wasn't coming back.

Lucky for me, I have always had a love affair with money. My older brother and I started mowing lawns for our neighbors when I was 9. I also babysat my newborn brother when I was 8 when my parents wanted a night out, and I continued babysitting him and other children until I was 14, which was when I was legally old enough to get a "real" job.

I then went to work at the local library shelving books, and I was soon promoted to head page and book mender. I also tutored other kids in math, algebra, geometry, English, and Spanish. Between my odd jobs and my frugal ways, I had managed to accumulate over $1,500 in a savings account by the time my mother decided to kick me out of the house forever.

As my new reality set in, I found a cheap, slum-like apartment owned by a kindly black lady in a very scary part of town. She happily took my money and didn't ask for any identification. Good thing since I didn't have any! I was terrified most of the nights during the few months I lived there. It was great being away from Psycho-Mom, but I was still only a young girl, afraid of bugs and the dark. I had only my clothes to my name. I didn't even own any towels, so I had to dry off from the shower with my bathrobe each day.

Things didn't get better anytime soon.

The first time I did laundry on my own, I figured the best way to get my clothes the cleanest was to set the washer on *hot*, and I thought it would be cheapest to put everything into one big load. I did the same thing with the dryer. After that, all my clothes were sort of grayish-colored and way too tight. Oops!

Another problem that began to show itself was one I'd actually had all my life - I suffered from low blood sugar. I used to faint from it ever since I was a little girl. Of course, I didn't realize it back then, since I was never actually diagnosed until I was in my early twenties. But when I tried to save money by eating only one meal a day (usually a box of donuts – *very* nutritious!) my hypoglycemia kicked in and I felt sick. I also gained an extra 35 pounds. It was a neat trick, stuffing my chunky self into my shrunken clothes!

I continued to attend high school, although I never

opened a book or did any homework again. I slept through most of my classes since I was always malnourished and exhausted. The long walk to and from school everyday and work every night really wiped me out. I don't know how I managed to stay in class. Looking back, I should have quit. School didn't do me any good in the long run. I could have used the time to rest, or to get a part-time job to earn more money. I even considered it once, briefly. But two things stopped me. First, I always loved learning, loved school and loved my teachers. Second, school was the only normal thing I had going in my life.

So I plodded along, following the same pattern, for as long as I could. And then one day, my doting mother went to my school principal's office and tried to get me expelled, telling him that I didn't live at her house anymore, and my new address put me out of their district. The administration ignored her, thankfully, since I had always been a favorite of all my teachers.

In time, I found a boyfriend, Jerry, who came from the most wonderful family I've ever known. They showed me what real love and affection were and what a happy family is like, and bless them, for they fed me dinner every night while their son and I dated.

Jerry was the son of a good friend of my mother. So, when mom went to their house one day and threatened to have him arrested and put in jail for statutory rape, I was stunned. She didn't really care whether or not he and I were actually having sex, she just wanted to make sure I didn't have anyone to care for me. She wanted to destroy me. And she tried her best to do so.

Thankfully, my surrogate family laughed in her face and showed her the door.

But that wasn't the end of things. The worst thing my mother did to me was to refuse to allow me any contact with my little brother. On my one day off of work each week, I used to walk to his neighborhood where he was outside playing so I could visit him. No one had told him I'd been kicked out. My mother simply said that I was "working late" whenever he asked about me. I guess she got my father and older brother to play along. Once she found out I'd been visiting him, she forbade him to see me or speak to me again. What could he do? He was afraid of being seen with me for fear of being punished.

Finally, my mother had found a way to hit me where I lived. I was devastated, thinking I would never see him again.

I'm not telling you all this so you will feel sorry for me. I don't ever want that. I'm telling you these things so that you will know that *anyone* can do what I did. No one bankrolled me, no one granted me any favors, no one loaned me a dime. I did everything on my own, and I made it. And if a kid with my background could, anybody can. And that means you can too!

After graduating high school, I moved to another state. My crazy family was moving hundreds of miles away to start life anew, and I just couldn't continue living in the same town where they had abused me so. I know family counselors say that running away is never a solution. In my case, it was. I needed to be in a place with no sad memories. I needed to be at peace.

So I moved to a brand new city and found another minimum-wage job working at a fast-food restaurant. As it did throughout most of high school, working in a food establishment guaranteed me a minimum of two semi-healthy meals a day. And I finally had some extra money to buy some groceries. I had roommates, so expenses weren't too bad, compared to having my own place in high school, but still, my budget was very tight.

But I was beginning to clear my head. I was starting to look at life without the constant destructive behavior of my family around me. Now that I was finally beginning to crawl out of survival mode, I began to wonder - how did I get *here*? I had always been told that I could do anything in life. So the question that plagued me most was: *What happened to my life???*

After all, this wasn't how I was supposed to end up. I was sure of that. But my liberal arts education had prepared me for nothing in the real world. I didn't know how to do laundry, I didn't know how to cook, I didn't know how to clean. I didn't know how to write a resume or how to dress for a job interview or anything useful. I didn't even know how to pay my own taxes. I threw the first three years of W-2 forms I ever received in the trash. It wasn't until I started dating Jerry and saw him filling out his tax returns that I asked his dad why those forms were so important. At first he was amused - and then when he realized I was serious, he taught me what I needed to know. It was a good thing, too, since I received a big tax refund from Uncle Sam that year, around $1,700. It seemed to me like a million!

While I was pondering the mediocrity of my existence, I received a letter in the mail from my birth mother. Remember when I mentioned I'd been adopted? She had managed to track me down when I was 18 and sent me a letter. I was delighted to finally have a mother who said she actually wanted me.

She invited me to come live with her and her family and offered to put me through college. I accepted eagerly, looking forward to a brand new home filled with love and acceptance. I figured college could only help, particularly since I had always enjoyed learning.

Well, as things turned out, I did manage to squeeze one semester in, although I had to pay for it myself through Pell Grants and testing out of classes. But I didn't get my happy ending. Nope. Instead, I received an emotionally damaged woman who lied to me at every turn.

She claimed she had become pregnant with me while being stabbed and raped by a stranger who left her for dead. I found out 10 years later that it was a complete fabrication. She not only knew who my birth father was, but also she had me baptized and his name placed on the baptismal certificate!

While I lived there, her husband was openly resentful and frequently tried to get me to leave the house. I had a half-brother and a half-sister whom I looked forward to embracing and loving, but my stepfather told them I was only a distant relative and I was forced to live that lie the entire time I was there. That didn't go over well with me, but I was trapped, even if only temporarily. I had no job, no car, no other place to go. Not that the car mattered all that much. I was 18 and still didn't know how to drive!

I had about $300 left from my last job, money I had been keeping for emergencies. I suddenly decided that my hostile living environment qualified. So I booked a flight to Dallas, to visit my dad where he had moved with the same girlfriend who had inspired him to abandon his family and responsibilities.

As things turned out, I found my dad's girlfriend to be a big step up from both my adopted and birth mothers. She was warm and outgoing and friendly. And, seeing as we were only three years apart, we had a lot in common and lots of fun together. She was like the older sister I'd never known.

She got me a job as a temp in her office at an insurance agency. They paid me the exorbitant salary of $750 a month. I felt absolutely rich, since that was nearly double what I had been used to making. They hired me full time, and I called my birth mother and told her to send my remaining clothes to me, because I wasn't coming back.

I worked at the insurance agency for a year-and-a-half. They had no dress code there, so I could go to work in my jeans and tee shirts and sneakers. Which was perfect! I loved the new friends I made at the office. Life was actually beginning to feel like fun. I had some extra money in my pocket, and a little bit of a social life.

I began my new career as a policy typist and was quickly promoted to insurance underwriter for the high-risk auto department. During that time, I gained my first real experience as a landlord. I found a new boyfriend, and he needed a place to live, since his old roommates had been stealing money from him. I suggested he move into my two-bedroom apartment (I already had one roommate to split the bills). He was agreeable, and we decided he would pay me $100 a month plus his fair share of the utilities.

Then more good news. He said he had a buddy who needed a place to stay, so I told him his friend could sleep on the couch for another $100 a month plus his share of the utilities. Then his buddy announced that he had a friend who needed a place to stay, so he ended up sleeping on the living room floor for yet another $100 a month plus utilities.

Suddenly I found myself living high on the hog—my boyfriend and I shared the master bedroom, so we had our privacy. My new roommates were bringing in more money than the total monthly amount for the rent on the apartment, and the utilities were paid by everyone else. I started joking about renting out the patio, insisting that for a guy looking out over the railing, it featured a half bath!

Before long, I was banking practically my entire paycheck and feeling great. I was well fed, well loved, and saving up money. After where I had begun my life, everything seemed to be going well.

Eventually, though, my boyfriend and I broke up, the roommates moved out, and my happy little insurance agency was bought out by another, larger firm. My new employer established a dress code and expected me to conform. Still being a teenager, my common sense was overridden by my youth, and I didn't want to spend my hard earned money on clothes that I would never wear except at work. So I did the only logical thing my teenaged brain could think of - I quit! After all, I had some money in the bank, so I could afford to treat myself to a little down time.

By now I was 19 and had finally learned to drive – my former boyfriend had taught me before we'd broken up. I had also acquired my very first car, a 1975 Dodge Duster – a real junker with no a/c, no paint, and slashed seats. But it ran well enough, and it was paid for, so I was happy.

While I was enjoying my unpaid vacation from work, I mentioned to my roommate that it would be nice to get money in the mail each day, instead of going out and working for it. If only I could figure out how to make that happen!

Well, that was the first germ of an idea that would eventually change my life.

Money in the mail, money in the mail, if only I could figure out how to make that happen...

I'd always been a firm believer that, if you can think it, if you can dream it, if you can say it, you can do it.

Of course, it didn't happen right away, but I hung onto

that thought - money in the mail - and I came back to it often. It swam around in my brain constantly - when I went out on a date, when I went dancing, while I ate, and even while I slept. That little thought had grown to become part of me, and my brain learned to watch for opportunities. Always watch for opportunities...

Throughout those early years on my own, from age 15 to 19, I was already learning, already planning, and already preparing for my future.

I learned that you truly only have three real needs in life - food, clothing, and shelter. Everything else is just gravy. I also learned that I'd never earn what I knew I was worth by working for others.

And I also knew that I really loved being a landlord and wanted to do it again someday.

Best of all, I came to realize that POVERTY SUCKS!, and it was time to change my life.

I started my first business when I was 20 years old. Since then, I have owned four more, one of which was renting out real estate again. I started all my businesses from scratch and sold them when they no longer excited me. I officially retired when I was 38. My goal had been to retire by the time I was 40. I beat the game. I made it.

Today, money just magically shows up in my mailbox. I don't ever have to go out and earn it again. Money in the mail – I finally figured out how to make it happen.

I also figured out something else - I am well qualified to give you advice. And the time for doing so has never been better.

So the only question I have is this:

Are *you* ready to become a self-made millionaire?

CHAPTER TWO

***I'll Try*, *I Can't*, and Other Things Losers Love to Say**

When people who are confronted with a problem say *I'll try*, what they're actually saying is that they doubt that they can resolve it. They're expecting failure. And it becomes a self-fulfilling prophecy.

People who say *I can't* are even worse. They have already come to the conclusion that success, for them, is an impossibility. When people say *I can't*, what they really mean is *I doubt that I can, so I won't even try*. And that's merely *another* way of setting oneself up for failure.

Let's face it. Life is filled with winners, and life is filled with whiners. And whiner is just another word for loser.

How do I define a loser? A loser is someone who approaches life with a negative attitude, someone who would rather go through life complaining than *ever* taking steps to make his situation better.

But that's not the end to it.

A loser loves to lay the blame for his failure outside of himself – on other people, outside forces, "bad luck," evil tides, or whatever seems handy at the moment. Losers *never* take personal responsibility for the problems they create. Oh, no. It's always someone else's fault. "Because of that other guy..."

But the fault lies within *them*.

We all make mistakes and take wrong turns in life. I don't blame anyone for doing that, because that's how people learn. I've made more than my fair share of mistakes over the years. But once you realize that you have turned your life into crap, it's time to pick up a shovel, scoop up the mess, and put it in the garbage can before kicking it out to the curb. It's no one else's job but yours.

"In Me We Trust"

The first business I ever founded was with a partner. I didn't have enough self-confidence to do it on my own, and Kathy was anxious to grab a piece of the good life, so we seemed like a natural fit.

We opened a business modeling lingerie for bar patrons. I thought it would be a big hit, since I felt Kathy was beautiful, and I thought I was pretty enough to get by. But I soon found out my partner smoked dope and did other drugs and had a deadbeat boyfriend sponging off her. Sound like a dream come true?

We had agreed that I would fund the business to the tune of $1,000, and she would pay me back $500 over time from each show we worked. Of course, she never paid me a nickel, plus I was the only one doing the marketing and cold-calling to line up the jobs. We took on a third model, Kathy's sister Denise, whom I also thought was beautiful - both of them much prettier than me. Still, after every show, we ended up getting fired. Whenever I asked the lounge managers why, I'd get the runaround. It was driving me crazy.

Finally, the last time it happened, I asked the lounge manager why once again, and she blew me away with her answer. She said "Aimee, you're really beautiful, but your other models are ugly! Get some prettier girls, come on back, and I'll be happy to hire you again."

I immediately dismantled our partnership and re-launched the business under a new name as sole owner. And it proved to be very successful.

Lesson Learned

The lesson I learned from that experience, of course, is to beware of partners with no money - not only will they screw you financially, but also they'll never, ever pull their own weight when it comes to doing the work. In fact, stay away from partners completely. Instead, believe in yourself. Whatever your insecurities are, whatever talents you think you lack, you can always hire someone else on a part-time basis to do that aspect of the work for you. In that way, if it turns out that your workers suck, you can fire them on the spot and hire someone else. A partner, on the other hand, can't be fired. A partner needs to be divorced, much like a spouse, which is a legal boondoggle and a very costly nightmare.

Another disaster I experienced in placing my faith in a business partner involved a heavy drinking ex-boyfriend who had cheated on me the entire time we had dated. He had owned a nightclub, which I found exciting, but he sold it shortly after we began going together. After we broke up and went our separate ways, he got back in touch with me. He wanted to open another nightclub, and he knew I had accumulated a tidy amount in savings. Would I go into partnership with him?

I asked to see the books of his prior business, and he promised to get them for me, but he never did. He told me that they were with his son in Las Vegas, while the club we were thinking of opening was in Texas.

It never dawned on me that his CPA (certified public accountant) was in Texas, and he would have had all the financials. Nevertheless, fully "trusting" the man, I went along with him. After all, cheating is always a sign of integrity, isn't it?

Before long, I discovered that Jonathan's greatest asset in running a bar consisted of his enormous capacity to hold his liquor and his enjoyment of giving away free drinks to his buddies. Whenever I tried to offer a suggestion to make the bar more profitable, he'd yell and scream at me until I backed down.

By the time I realized the gravity of my mistake, we were already incorporated in an equal partnership. Thankfully, my gut instincts had prompted me to take the title of corporate president, which gave me a split millimeter more power than my partner had by law. I was soon going to need it.

We had each agreed to put up $10,000 in cash to fund the business. Jonathan quickly ran out of funds, which he'd been drawing off his credit card. So I was forced to sink still more of my savings into a steadily growing money pit. Within months we were deep in debt. Jonathan started talking about filing for bankruptcy, which was fine for him, since he hadn't invested his own money in the place and had no tangible assets. I still had about $30,000 in the bank and I wanted to keep it. So I managed to legally fire him from the business and continue on alone. It took me three months to break even. The fourth month, I turned a profit, and with that, I quickly sold the place for $15,000.

Another lesson well learned. After that experience, I vowed never again to have a business partner. Same lesson as in Story # 1 – only considerably more costly.

My "Rule of Five"

So I learned five valuable lessons from my first two unsuccessful forays into the world of business:

    1. Never have a partner.

    2. Never have retail space.

    3. Never lack confidence in yourself.

    4. Only do a business that produces residual income.

    5. Only do a business that allows you to hire someone else who can duplicate your work.

Those are lessons I've never forgotten, and lessons I'm going to burn into your brain before we're through.

CHAPTER THREE

***I Will, I Can*, and Other Things Winners Have to Say**

Everybody loves a winner. But more to the point, everybody loves to be around a winner. And why not? Winners teach us how to get the best out of life. They teach us how to be successful, how to enjoy what we're doing with our lives, how to prosper.

But what, exactly, is a winner? I believe a winner is someone who is always willing to find a way around any obstacle in his path. He's someone who doesn't give up until he succeeds. He's someone who *will*.

When someone says *I will*, he's made a decision to succeed at whatever he's chosen to do. He's determined, confident, and above all tenaciously persistent.

I once asked my dad a business question because I needed the answer for an issue of my own. He didn't respond, so every couple of days, I called him about it. That's when he labeled me "tenaciously persistent." I told him he was being redundant. He responded with much aggravation, "No, Aimee, I'm not. When you decide to go after something, you're like a pit bull. You grab hold and you don't let go until you get what you want, and then you *still* won't let go. Persistent does not *begin* to describe you. You are *tenaciously* persistent, and I am *not* being redundant!"

He was quite angry and trying to bully me into leaving him alone. But even though he was annoyed by me, the underlying message he sent me was that I was a winner! While he didn't like dealing with me, he had just acknowledged that I accomplish what I decide to do – no matter what! And that absolutely delighted me.

The Meaning of *I Can*

Similarly, when someone says *I can*, he's simply making another form of commitment to what he's doing. *I will* means you will do whatever you're talking about. *I can* means you're physically or mentally capable of doing it and that you will succeed.

When I was first kicked out of the house, I never questioned my ability to take care of myself and fix my life. I simply believed without any hesitation or doubt whatsoever that somehow, someway, I would and I could take care of myself.

And I was correct, as it turned out. I survived and I eventually thrived. All because I decided that I would.

Stay Focused!

I also believe that being a winner means living your own life in your own way. That means doing what's important to *you* – not doing things to impress others.

For me, buying into an early retirement and never having to worry about being homeless or hungry again were what mattered most to me. Having happy, healthy relationships with the people I allow into my life is a treasure beyond measure to me.

Do what's right for *you*, and have the courage of your convictions!

Persistence Pays Off!

If something is important enough to you, don't quit! There are plenty of geniuses in the world today, plenty of talented, brilliant people who have no success in their lives. That's because being a winner is not about having brains. It's about not giving up. Ever. Go after what you want, don't listen to losers who want you to fail so that they'll look good by comparison. Surround yourself with people who are positive and encouraging.

Persistence always pays off. I believe persistence plus an unwavering belief in yourself are the two most important qualities you can have as a winner.

I learned early on that life wasn't fair. It's one of the best lessons I ever learned, because it was one of the truest. When you can accept that sometimes life is unfair, you learn to stop taking things personally. Sometimes life knocks you down for no apparent reason, and other times you get windfalls - of money, or wonderful people, or opportunities. So I keep my eyes open and watch for the windfalls. And I stay as prepared as possible for the occasional setbacks.

Today, as before, whenever life bombards me with an unpleasant surprise, I face it head on. While it may be difficult at times, I have never regretted doing so. You simply can't give up if you want to be a winner.

In my early years on my own, my dad used to say that he never worried about me, because I was a "survivor." I know he meant it as a compliment, but I took great offense at the time, because I didn't want to merely survive. I wanted to thrive, to be something better, to grow. But I didn't know how to get from Point A (I had grown into a chubby, broke, exhausted loser in a dead-end job) to Point B. Heck, I didn't even know what Point B was! I had just about given up any hope that I'd ever had for a better life, and suddenly I received that letter from my birth mother. At last, I was going to make something of myself. I had found my Point B!

Even though things didn't work out quite the way I'd hoped, they opened up other avenues to me, and in the end everything panned out perfectly.

Eternally Optimistic

Being an eternal optimist my entire life, it never enters my mind that I will ever fail at anything I try. I'm not always right – I have failed occasionally *and* made plenty of mistakes on my road to financial freedom. But my eternal optimism always makes me believe absolutely in my ability to succeed. And as my success with my businesses grew, so did my confidence. And so will yours!

Now, let's get on to the nitty-gritty of this book. Let's start turning you into a real financial winner!

CHAPTER FOUR

How to Decide Which Business is Right for You

It's clear that the concepts of *I will* and *I can* are necessary in forming a winning attitude, but those two phrases can also provide you with yet another weapon in your arsenal leading to financial independence. They can act as a reminder that there are many ways to handle any unusual business situation.

In every business I've ever gotten into, I started out by doing as much research as I possibly could before actually starting the business. I couldn't possibly learn everything about the business, of course. But I always do my research as thoroughly as I can, and I ask myself a series of questions.

Does this business excite me? If the answer is *no*, I move on. If the answer is *yes*, I ask several more questions. *How can I make money from this business? What are the expenses going to be? What can I expect my income to be? What are the start up costs?* (I always like them to be low,

low, *low!*)

Then I ask more. *Is there residual income to be made off this business? Can I run the business from my home? Can I replace myself by hiring employees, so that I can concentrate on growing the business? How much competition is there in this field where I live?*

The Importance of Residual Income

Residual income is money that you earn from selling the customer *just once,* then you keep receiving money week after week, month after month, year after year on that one single sale. An example of a business that produces lots of residual income is an insurance agent. He sells you *just once* – when he signs you up for your new policies for auto, homeowner, life, health and possibly disability insurance. That one-time, one hour appointment is *all* the work he has done, and then he gets commission on that first time sale – and *every year* after that he continues to receive commissions on *all* your renewal policies – but he hasn't done any extra work for *any* of your renewal business. That's how "residual" income works. It's a client you line up *once,* and then you make money off that same client for years and years to come with no extra effort.

An example of "non-residual" income would be a car salesman. He sells you a car *once*, and he likely won't ever see you again. Unless he stays at the same dealership (unlikely), and you stay loyal to the car brand and never try out another brand (also unlikely), the car salesman knows he won't be seeing you again. No residual commission here, just lots of "one-time only" sales.

With non-residual income, you have to work hard and earn every dollar you make. You have to sell each new customer, because you never see the same customer twice. And because of this, your income potential is limited by the number of business hours in your day, and the number of clients you successfully sell each day.

With residual income, you can work very little and make a lot of money. Because you sell your customer only once, and then the money keeps rolling in again and again and again. So your income potential is unlimited. So when selecting the business that's right for you, if it doesn't offer residual income, I don't care how excited you are, it's not going to be the right business for you if you want to retire early. Always, always, *always* choose a business with residual income.

Running Your New Business from Your Home

As you'll see in a later chapter on "running the numbers," it's critically important to select a business that you can run from your own home. Because you don't know how slow or how fast your new business will grow, you don't want to burden yourself with the exorbitant cost of retail space. And even if your business is making you wheel barrels full of dead presidents, do you really want to throw a large portion of it away on overhead?

Overhead is typically made up of the following costs: the cost of renting commercial space, paying the property taxes on the building, paying for insurance on the building you rent and an inflated commercial liability insurance policy on that building - both policies are to protect the landlord, by the way, not you! Other overhead costs include paying for maintenance of the parking lot and landscaping, paying for maintenance and repairs on the building you are renting, paying for special licenses, permits, and possibly sales taxes associated with your new business. Some commercial leases also have annual rent hikes built in, as well as demanding a percentage of your gross income!

You'll also have to deal with paying for building inspectors, the cost of business furniture and equipment, any inventory required, and paying for any signs you want for your business. You'll pay for sewer and trash and electric and water and possibly gas in this commercial property. All of these expenses add up so quickly and in such large amounts that you could be committed to several thousand dollars going out the door *each and every month* – regardless of how much money is coming in!

So don't get caught up in wanting a fancy office or storefront for your new business. It will stress you to the max trying to meet the monthly bills, cost you a small fortune, and possibly even cost you your early retirement. If you can't run your new business out of your home, then I say move on – to a more profitable business that will be a financial winner – not a financial drain!

Replace Yourself!

It's vitally important that you select a business that allows you to hire employees to do the work for you. If you have to handle every service yourself, you will never be able to grow your business into anything larger than just one service route. And that will never make you rich or able to retire.

The business you choose must be simple enough for you to be able to hire people to replace you. If you can't foresee employees taking over the service role, then you need to select another business.

Interviewing the Competition

When contemplating a new business venture, I *always* interview the competition, pretending I'm a potential customer, to gather more information. I try to find out how *they* conduct business. *How do they dress for new client interviews? How much do they charge for their services? What is their presentation like? Do I believe I can operate the same business as well as or better than my competition? Can I find as many customers as they can?*

Picking a Winner

After I have examined my possible new business venture, and see there is residual income to be made, that I can run it from home, that I can replace myself, and that I can outshine the competition, then I ask myself some more questions: *What is the likely growth pattern I see for this business? How long do I want to keep the business? What is my exit strategy if it goes well? And what if it goes poorly?*

In short, I plan for the worst case scenario and hope for the best. After asking myself these questions and coming up with the answers, I dig deep down inside and ask myself, *Am I even more excited about this business than I was before?* If my answer is *yes,* that's my signal to forge ahead and take that next step. But, if the answer is *no* or if I find myself dreading going into that business, I stop right there. If you don't have a passion for your new business venture, you won't succeed, because you won't find any joy in it. But if you're still excited and looking forward to taking the plunge, go for it!

Unexpected Surprises
Try to remember that, no matter how much planning, researching, and organizing you do beforehand, there will always be surprises - something you'll have no idea how to handle - at first.

It's happened to me in every new business I ever started. But my Winner Mentality tells me that's okay. That simply means I'll have to re-group, buy a little time, and learn something new.

Whatever you do, make sure you deliver whatever it is you promise your customer *when you promise it*. Under-promise and over-deliver rather than the other way around, and you'll end up with a satisfied customer forever. If you promise to deliver by no later than Friday, showing up on Thursday is a nice touch. Customer impressed! But promise to deliver no later than Friday and show up on Saturday with nothing but excuses, and you'll lose all credibility. And lost credibility equals lost customers, which translates to lost income.

Are You Smart Enough?
Sometimes people have the nagging feeling that they might not be smart enough to start and run a new business. That's rarely true. Even though school came easy for me, my high school diploma did nothing for me so far as financial success goes. I didn't need anything beyond a third-grade education to become successful at any of the businesses I founded. And neither do you. If you can read, write, and do basic math, if you have the motivation, determination, and self-discipline, and most of all the belief in yourself to succeed, you

can do it too.

It wasn't "book smarts" that made me a multi-millionaire. And it wasn't the "street smarts" I'd learned early in life.

It was my commitment to success.

Are you committed to success as well? Let's find out. Let's get you started on your way to financial independence, beginning with finding what it is you're going to love to do!

CHAPTER FIVE

Brainstorm Your Way to Success

What would I do to help you zero-in on your dream business if I was sitting across the table from you right now?

I would tell you to do exactly what I do. Here's a look into my continuing search for new and exciting businesses to start up. Although now I seek out new ventures because I *want* to and not because I *have* to.

I try to find things I enjoy doing when I'm not working - hobbies and other fun activities I get a kick out of. And then I figure out ways to make money from them. And there's *always* a way to make money from something you enjoy doing.

Make a List...

One of the first things I tell people who want to know what business they should get into is to brainstorm. Get a notepad and pen – or sit down at the word processor – and just start writing down or typing out everything that gives you pleasure in life. From hobbies and fun activities to just everyday plain silly stuff – absolutely *everything* that brings you joy, or even anything that you've never done but that you've always wanted to do or thought about trying to do.

After you have that list, try to figure out ways you can turn these hobbies and interests into money making service businesses. For some ideas, you may not be able to figure anything out, but if you brainstorm at least 50 interests onto your list, you should be able to come up with at least five simple, suitable, service businesses from the ideas listed. And out of those 5, as long as they meet the business criteria for my "Rule of Five," you should find at least one that gets you *really* excited!

If you are still stumped, the next chapter gives you a good size list of business ideas, so you may find one there that appeals to you. And the next chapter also helps you to train your brain to think in a new way to develop ideas to make money off of your hobbies and interests.

Bookstores and Internet Searches

If you still can't come up with a business idea between this chapter and Chapter Six, then I suggest you go to your local bookstore and skim through books containing subject matter on home based businesses. You can also go online and do an internet search for "home based businesses" and see what comes up. If those actions don't lead to any immediate excitement within you that is an indicator you may have just struck business gold, then I suggest that you don't worry, take your time, and explore some more. This is one of the most important decisions you will make in your life – it's perfectly fine to spend a few months searching out the right business for you.

Continuing Education

One avenue I took was to go to my local state and community colleges, and ask for their "continuing education" class catalogs. These are the "fun" classes for adults, and they generally aren't meant to lead to a degree of any kind. Read through the catalogs and see if anything piques your interest. If so, sign up for the classes. Go and see how you like the classes, and think about different ways that you can make a service business out of any of these new skills you have learned.

Is the subject matter something you can teach? Is it a skill (service) that you can sell to others for a fee on a regular basis? Is it something you really enjoy? Does the class teach you to turn out a really inexpensive but very high volume product that you can sell many times over for residual income?

Sometimes, investigating certain avenues for what turns out to be the wrong service business for you can lead you right onto the path of the one that's perfect for you.

Yellow Pages

You can also just search through the yellow pages in your phone book. Start at the letter "A" and work your way to "Z." Make a list of all the business ideas in there that sound interesting or fun or exciting to you. Some ideas are hard to come up with on your own, but when you see the good idea yourself – you feel that involuntary response in your excitement level - *that* could be just the right business for you!

However, I don't recommend that you pick the first business that intrigues you. Whatever method you use, make sure you are deciding between at least a few different ideas to find that perfect business for you. You want to have at least a couple of business ideas that really make you itch to do them. Then do your due diligence on the business ideas and make sure that *whichever* business you finally select fits my business criteria "Rule of Five."

You can also take your brainstorming list and if you are having trouble coming up with a workable service business from your list, look up each topic in the yellow page ads to see if there are any businesses already in existence for that topic. Or do an internet search using your hobby as one of the keywords in your search – for example type in "kites"+"home based business" and see what comes up on the web. You are very likely to come up with the business idea of your dreams using these techniques.

I've already told you about how I started my lingerie modeling business and my nightclub, so I won't review the details of those businesses again here.

But here are a couple of other examples from my own history:

After I had sold my lingerie business and my nightclub in Texas, I moved to Las Vegas. I got married, and didn't have to work for the first time in my life. I thought it would be relaxing, but I quickly grew bored and started searching for a new business venture. My first thought was to open a floral arranging business, as I thought it would be a "happy, feel-good" type of business. When I saw the tremendous amount of competition in the yellow pages, I knew in my gut it wouldn't work, and so I decided to regroup. I spent several months taking night classes and seminars at the local colleges, I read books on home based businesses, and I came across both the pet-sitting business and the indoor plant care business. I have always loved animals, and I have always had a green thumb, so both businesses seemed like a perfect fit for me.

I did my research on the pet-sitting business and I thought it sounded fun and easy. I was right. It followed my formula - low start up costs (under $1,000), residual income (get a customer once, and if he likes you, he'll use you over and over again). I loved the people and animals I met and befriended. It was very much a "feel good" business. I was happy going to work, I had no inventory to carry, and I had no overhead and no retail space to worry about, and I could hire workers to replace me. Who could ask for anything more?

At the same time that I started my pet-sitting business, I also started my indoor plant business, which also fit my business criteria "Rule of Five." The plant business was another simple business with no overhead and low start up costs (under $1,000 again), it offered residual income, I was able to replace myself by hiring workers to help me, and it was based on my love of caring for plants.

I figured that the plant business would be more profitable in the long run but grow more slowly. And that the pet-sitting business would grow more quickly but be less profitable in the long run. I was right about both businesses. And so I kept the pet-sitting business until my plant business took off, and then I sold my pet business as planned.

Nothing Lasts Forever

Remember, once you come up with a business with low overhead that can be run out of your home, that has residual income and low start up costs, where you can eventually replace yourself with another worker, you aren't locked into that business forever. The whole idea of starting a profitable service business from scratch is to run it for as long as you want and then either sell it for a profit or promote your best worker to manage it for you.

If you decide to sell, remember that no business is without value. The greater the income your service business generates, the more money you can sell it for later on. We'll talk more about selling your service business in a later chapter. And it's also perfectly acceptable to "retire" without selling your service business. You can promote your best and most suitable employee to manage your business for you. Just make sure that *you* retain control of the finances, and that your manager is thoroughly trained and capable of both maintaining and continuing to grow your business *before* you hand the reins over to him. And if you decide to sell your business, you can invest in either real estate or paper assets or both. Or you can keep your service business complete with manager, and *still* invest in real estate, paper assets or both. And I'll show you how to do all of it in later chapters. There is no wrong way to retire – any of these combinations can work for you. All of them can lead to you sailing off into your early retirement!

Always remember, just as there is always more than one way to solve unusual business situations, there is always more than one way to retire. It all depends on which way makes *you* feel the happiest, most comfortable and stress-free.

If you still haven't found the ideal service business for you, hang onto your lists that you made earlier in this chapter. Bring them with you to Chapter Six, and I'll show you more techniques on finding the right business for you. I'll also provide you with a large sampling of businesses that may just appeal to you – and they already fit my business criteria "Rule of Five," making your search that much easier!

CHAPTER SIX

Do What You Love

Do what you love and work will always feel like play!
That's my philosophy. And it's my philosophy because *it's true!* The only question is this: How do you find what you love to do?

I've given you a look into how I spend my search time when looking for a new business to found. Check out college courses, think about what you enjoy doing in your free time, make a list of everything that interests you.

You see, the easy part of "doing what you love to do" is doing what you love for fun. The harder part is figuring out how to turn your fun hobby into a successful business.

If You Had a Million Dollars...
You might ask yourself what you'd do if someone gave you a million dollars, tax free, tomorrow. What would you do? How would you spend your time and money?

The typical answer is also the simplest. "Well, I guess I'd pay off my house, car and any other debts and invest the rest for income. Then I'd quit my job. I'd live off the investment income so that I'd never have to worry about running out of money again. I'd travel. I'd go to the theater or concerts or sporting events or play golf or shop. I'd eat out at fancy restaurants. You know, just enjoy life."

But would that really be best for you in the long run? Or would your life still be missing something? You could do all those things, of course, and still feel a vacuum in your life. You'd be living the good life all right, but you wouldn't be enjoying it because you *still* wouldn't be doing what it is you love to do.

Bumming around or filling your life with empty activities might hold your interest for a while, but in the long run, you're going to crave to do something that's meaningful to *you!* But what? And how do you find out?

I developed a knack over the years for turning fun hobbies into money making businesses. I can find a great business opportunity in almost any enjoyable activity. You can, too. Doing so simply takes practice. It requires training yourself to ask the same questions over and over: *"How can I turn this into a money-making service business that I'd love to run?" "Can I run this business from my home?" "Are the start up costs low?" "Does this business provide residual income?"* And the most important question of all *"Can I duplicate myself by hiring someone else to do the work for me?"*

In all of the following examples, the service businesses fit my "Rule of Five" criteria. You are able to run the business from your home, the start up costs are low, the business can provide residual income, and you can duplicate yourself by hiring temps to do the service routes or client lists you develop. And best of all, no partners are required – or desired! Take a look at this list, and see if anything jumps out at you as something that you might just *love* to do...

Photography – Are you so in love with your camera that if it's not in your hand you feel like you are missing a few fingers? Weddings, pet portraits, family portraits – you keep ownership of the digital imagery and sell photo packages to all the family members. Portraits can be done annually, seasonally and for the holidays. Identity cards for children taken each year at school or daycare, for the parent to have ready for police in case the child is kidnapped. Includes age, height, weight, name and contact info of the child. Re-do identity cards every year of school until kids are safely grown into adults. Tons of residual income potential. Hire temps as your client list grows.

Bookkeeping – Do you enjoy playing with money and keeping it organized? Every time you get enough customers to keep you busy full time, you hire a full-time temp to cover that set of customers.

Pet Day Care – Do all animals notice the "sucker" tattoo on your forehead – the one that's only visible to our four-legged friends? (I have the same tattoo!) Done in the clients home when clients are on vacation or daily dog walking for people working all day. You hire temps to do the service for you.

Elderly Day Care – Do you love spending time with your own grandma and grandpa? Done in the clients home. Assist with all non-medical aspects of care – cleaning, cooking a meal and doing dishes, helping the senior to dress. Provide live-in or daily visits to people who are elderly, disabled or ill. You hire temps to do the service for you.

Pool Cleaning Service – Do you love feeling like a perpetual beach bum? Provide pool cleaning service at clients homes. Hire temps as you establish your routes, to do the work for you.

Computer Training / Trouble Shooting – Are you a techno-geek just dying to show off your mad computer skills? Help both individuals and businesses. Services to offer include repairs, training, networking, web design, web hosting, domain names and e-commerce solutions. Hire college kids who are computer experts *through* a temp agency or use the agency temps if they are skilled enough.

Companions for the Elderly and/or New Mothers – Are you social and love helping others? Done in the clients home. Provide transportation, shopping, doing errands, and companionship to new moms and / or the elderly. You hire temps to do the work for you.

Child Day Care – Are you a softie for little ones? Done in the clients home. Care for the children on a regular part-time basis or with full-time nannies. You hire temps to do the service for you.

Lawn Care Service – Do you love playing in your own garden and turning it into your own personal enchanted forest? Provide mowing, blowing, bagging up the debris, weeding, trimming bushes and trees, sprinkler monitoring and repair as needed. Hire temps to do the work for you as you repeatedly establish full-time service routes.

Handyman Service – Did you love taking things apart and putting them back together when you were a kid? If you have basic handyman skills, you'll know what each job entails and what to charge. Then you line up the jobs and hire temps to do the service routes for you.

Maid Service / Commercial Cleaning Service – Can't stand to see a speck of dust or an item out of place? Line up the jobs on a weekly or daily basis, and hire a crew of temps to do the jobs for you.

Indoor Plant Care Service – Do you love playing with plants but don't want to be outside in nasty weather? Sell or rent live and silk plants to your clients and provide service to both as well. Hire temps to do the service routes for you.

Vacant House Sitting – Do you have strong protective instincts? Done while the client is out of town to avoid thieves, vandals or the homeless breaking in. You hire temps to do the service for you.

Personal Shopping Service – Do you think the mall is the happiest place on earth? Provide personal shopping for people who are too rich, famous or busy to do it themselves. Brides can especially use a personal shopper. Hire temps to provide the service for you.

Holiday Decoration Rental Service – Are your Christmas decorations still up in July? Provide holiday decorations for rent to any type of business, such as hotels, banks, restaurants, malls, retirement homes, hospitals, car dealerships, doctors, lawyers, any type of office, even to private homes. Most months have at least one holiday in them, so you will have residual income every month. Hire temps to install the decorations and rotate them according to that particular holiday.

Door-to-Door Dry Cleaning – Do you want to rub elbows with people who are too rich to pick up their own dry cleaning? Provide pick up and delivery of dry cleaning, as well as shoes, suitcases, clothes and purses for repairs. Hire temps to do the service for you.

Ready To Do What You Love?
By now you should have several choice business ideas to choose from. You'll need to do a little more research into your top picks before deciding on your winning business idea. But what if you *still* haven't found your dream business? Well,

then it's time for some professional help – and it's *free!*

CHAPTER SEVEN

What to Do If You *Still* Can't Find the Right Business for You

Ok, so you've tried brainstorming, you've made all your lists, you've looked on the internet and in the yellow pages. You've looked at all the sample service businesses in the last chapter. You've thought of all the hobbies and interests and things you love to do, and you are still uninspired. You've taken classes and read books on service business ideas. You just can't come up with what feels like the "right" business for you. Or perhaps you've thought of a business or two, but they don't meet the criteria for my "Rule of Five:"

1. Never have a partner.

2. Never have retail space.

3. Never lack confidence in yourself.

4. Only do a business that produces residual income.

5. Only do a business that allows you to hire someone else who can duplicate your work.

So what do you do now? Well, you've already learned how self-defeating the words "I'll try" and "I can't" are, so you aren't even going to think those words. You are *not* going to give up. Quitting is *not* an option! You are going to be the winner that I *know* you can be, you are going to be the person who says "I will" and "I can" and you *are* going to find the business that's right for you. But now we're going to get you some professional help – and that help is going to be *free of charge!*

Professional Help

That professional who is going to assist you is called a "business broker." You can look up business brokers online or in the yellow pages. Just like a CPA, attorney, real estate agent or any other professional you deal with, you are going to interview them and find who is most suitable for you to work with. You want to settle on someone who is both honest and trustworthy, has great expertise in his field, and best of all is someone whom you enjoy working with.

Interview Your Brokers

First of all, you want to make sure that there are *no fees to you* for his service. Much like a real estate agent, a *legitimate* business broker will charge *nothing* to the buyer. The seller pays the business broker a commission upon the successful completion of the business sale. If you find a broker who tries to charge you all kinds of "garbage fees," run for the hills. Typically, garbage fees are things like a fee to evaluate the type of business you want to buy or to charge you a consultation fee for meeting with you. Another garbage fee might be a charge for showing you his available portfolio of businesses. Or a fee to set up a meeting between you and the sellers. Basically any type of fee that a business broker would want to charge you, as a buyer, is a garbage fee.

If any broker tried the garbage fee scam on me, I would do one of two things. I might stand up and walk right out of his office. Or, if he had a business for sale that was of great interest to me, which as you know by now is not always that easy to come by, I would look him dead in the eye and smile and possibly chuckle a little and say calmly but firmly, "I don't pay garbage fees, but I do admire your chutzpah for trying. So now, are we going to get down to legitimate business, or am I going to leave your office and deal with a broker who *doesn't* think I'm so inexperienced that I would pay garbage fees?"

You want to be firm, calm, and just a touch humorous in your statement. Because if your broker is going to back down off of his garbage fees, you have to allow him a way to do it while still saving face. If you just bully or browbeat him or yell at him, you will only alienate him and he won't want to give you his best efforts. But by phrasing it like I did above, you have actually complimented him. After all, you just told him you admired his chutzpah, which business people *love* to hear! And by being calm, you have shown him that you didn't take it personally, so that lets him know there are no hard feelings, so he won't be embarrassed by working with you. Which is important, because embarrassment or humiliation *never* produces good results in a business relationship. And by smiling or laughing just a little during your little speech, you allow him to make a joke of it, as if he wasn't really serious, just kidding, ha ha. Which allows him to save face. And now he also knows that you didn't just fall off the turnip truck yesterday. You have earned his respect, and it's unlikely he will try any other devious tricks on you now, because he knows you're wise to them.

However, all that being said, I would still watch this guy like the proverbial hawk, to make sure he doesn't try anything else funny later on. Of course, whomever you deal with, even if you 100% trust in their integrity, you should always, always, *always* be reading every contract and asking questions until you understand *everything*. And then still showing it to your lawyer for a final review before signing anything. You are *never* to take anyone's word for the fairness or correctness of any contract. You always need to protect yourself by reading every contract you sign, no matter what the business situation.

The SBA is Your Friend!

The second thing I would look for in a business broker is someone who has good connections with the SBA (Small Business Administration). This is an organization that finances loans for business purchases. Think of them as a mortgage broker on your house, only they are loaning money for business sales. If your business broker can walk you through the process rather painlessly because he has a good connection, that can be tremendously helpful. Trying to go through all the government red tape on your own may just lead you to great frustration, however, which you don't need!

NDAs (Non Disclosure Agreements) and Non-Competes

Now, unless you find a business you would like to buy from the business broker, it's unlikely he would ask you to sign anything other than an "NDA" (Non-Disclosure Agreement.) That is to protect the seller. Just like when you get ready to sell your business later on down the road, you won't want it advertised to the world, because it can destroy your business and you'll have nothing left to sell. You don't want anyone to know it's for sale until after it's sold, a done deal.

And here is why: If your employees know you are trying to sell your business, they may start looking for a new job and quit. Or if it's a cash business they may start stealing from you, thinking that you will be gone soon and therefore you either won't notice or won't care. Or they may start slacking off on their jobs since "the boss" will soon be gone. And worse yet, if your clients were to find out you were looking to sell, they would likely start looking for someone to replace you. They will feel like you are abandoning them and no longer care about them, so their loyalty to you will disappear. And then if they find a new servicer, all the value of your business will disappear as well. All of which not only makes your business less valuable for sale, it could destroy it completely. So signing an NDA is perfectly acceptable and actually expected when you are a buyer working with a business broker. You will want the same confidentiality from your prospective buyers when you get to the point of selling your own business. So remember that for later!

One more point to remember on the NDA – make sure it doesn't say anyplace on it that you are "forbidden" from starting a similar business to any that are shown to you. That's a Non-Compete Agreement. It's actually very unlikely that you would be asked to sign a non-compete at this stage of the game, since you won't be provided with any business names yet, until and unless you have made an offer to purchase the business in question. If your broker does want you to sign a non-compete agreement, just refuse to sign and just tell the broker that until you settle on a definite business that you would like to make an actual offer on, you aren't looking for any confidential information, and don't even need to know the name of any particular business for sale, so there is no need for a confidentiality agreement (NDA) or a non-compete to be signed at this time. Don't let yourself be bullied on this point. Business brokers usually have way more businesses for sale than they have qualified buyers. So they will go along with pretty much whatever you want, just as long as you aren't trying to get confidential or proprietary information without an NDA or a non-compete agreement if there is an actual deal on the table.

No Exclusivity

Also, just like a real estate agent, a business broker may try to get you to sign an "exclusive" agreement to work only with him. Don't sign it! Absolutely refuse! Also refuse to sign this type of document for a real estate agent. Just as with a business broker or real estate agent, in case your guy bombs or you find you can't stand working with him, then you are free to leave him and work with another agent or broker.

If you are unable to find a suitable business from that particular broker, you also want to be free to use other brokers to find your dream business. A business broker is a little different than a real estate agent. A real estate agent has listings that are put on the listing service for *all* other real estate agents and brokers in town to see and share – as it greatly increases their ability to sell. But business brokers tend to keep all their listings to themselves – in house. So every broker has something different to offer. So you want to be free to shop at every business broker's house if you want to!

So now that you have found legitimate, trustworthy business brokers out there, and you have possibly both read *and* signed their NDAs, now those brokers will allow you to look at their inventory – which means the businesses that they have for sale. You'll be surprised at what type of businesses are available for sale – everything you can imagine – and everything you can't! But it's likely that you'll find at least one business that piques your interest *and* that meets my business criteria "Rule of Five." Ask the business broker as many questions as you can about how the business works, how it makes money, is there any overhead, how many employees are involved, how much money is it taking in and what type of expenses does it have?

Excellent! Now we're making progress. And now there are two ways you can go. The first is to start this business from scratch on your own. In the following chapter I explain how to run the numbers to figure out how much it will cost to start your own new business. I also go over all the steps you will need to take to start it up. And I teach you how to grow it successfully and easily. So long as you have your business idea and know what you want to do, you can continue to follow the formula in my book and you'll do just fine, without buying a ready-made business from a broker. And since you haven't seen the owners books or customer list, and you haven't signed a non-compete agreement, you are in the clear. And as long as you honor the terms of the confidentiality agreement or NDA, you will not have violated any legally binding agreements.

However, you do also have another option. This option will work best if you already have some money in the bank and reasonably good credit. But it can also work if you have no money in the bank and fairly decent credit. You can also just *buy* the ready-made business from the seller. Where there is a will, there are always *so many ways* to succeed!

While I'm not a huge fan of debt (other than mortgages for rental properties), if you are comfortable enough, you can certainly buy your business already up and running. And you can finance the purchase. The lady who purchased my plant business through the business broker is still doing great with it ten years later. All my prior customers love her, and she has expanded way beyond what I had done with it. She is much more aggressive than I ever was in the marketing department, and she has certainly reaped the rewards. And good for her!

And good for you as well? Let's run some numbers and find out...

Let's say that you find a business that is up for sale that is netting right at $20,000 a month profit after all expenses, but before taxes, to keep the numbers simple.

Let's say that you purchase that business for $125,000. If the SBA requires you to put 10% down, that means you would need to come up with $12,500 as a down payment. However, the SBA will sometimes allow the seller to "carry the paper" (that means the seller loans you the other 5% and you pay him back over time as well) for approximately 5% of the loan. So you may only need to come up with a 5% down payment of your own money, or $6,250.

So let's see how that shakes out, both ways...

Example # 1 – You pay the full 10% down payment of $12,500. The loan balance is now $112,500. At a normal 8% interest rate, your monthly payment is just $1,365 a month! And bear in mind, the term (length of time) of an SBA loan is usually just 10 years. So you'll own the business free and clear after *only* ten years. And from *day one* you'll be making $18,635 a month in profits!!!

To determine your return on investment (ROI), you take the $12,500 (your initial investment) and divide that number into your annual return of $223,620 ($18,635 a month profit times 12 months in a year). That means your ROI is 1,788.96% - and that is a phenomenal rate of return! Most people would be delighted to get 7% - 8% in any investment in today's market. 12% is considered huge. But 1,788.96% return is absolutely astronomical in any market. And deals like this can be found – business owners get sick, they retire, they die, they move away to care for a loved one, or like me and my plant business they can have a car accident that causes them to sell at a huge discount just to get rid of a highly successful business.

Example # 2 – You pay just 5% down payment of $6,250. Your seller carries 5% of the loan balance at an 8% interest rate and the SBA carries the rest of the loan balance of the same $112,500, also at an 8% interest rate. And again, the term for both the SBA loan and your loan with the seller is just 10 years. Now out of your $20,000 in profits every month, you are still paying $1,365 a month to the SBA, and you will pay $76 a month to the seller of the business. Which leaves you with a net profit before taxes of $18,559 each month. And now your ROI is considerably higher, because your initial investment was only $6,250 and your annual return is now $222,708 (18,559 a month profit times twelve months). Divide your annual return of $222,708 by your initial investment of $6,250, and now your ROI is 3,563.32% - and that's virtually twice the return as before!

And the numbers used above are roughly the same numbers from my plant business sale, just so that you know for a fact that deals like this are absolutely possible!

What If You Don't Have the Down Payment or Your Credit is "Iffy"

If you decide you want to buy a ready-made business, and you don't already have the down payment and/or your credit is "iffy" – what do you do? You actually do have several options that can still make this work. Remember, "I will" and "I can" – so if you want something, don't give up until you get it!

On the down payment, you have several options.

Especially if you are only looking at a down payment of $6,250 or $12,000. First of all, you can go get a second job and earn the money and save it up. It won't take that long, and as I explain later on, most businesses for sale don't have that many buyers making offers because most people are employees, not business owners. So for any business to sell takes some time, usually a year or two, and they don't often get many offers to choose from during that time.

But if the seller just won't wait, you can also see about borrowing your initial down payment from a friend or family member. Paying them back at the same rates listed above means either an extra $76 or $152 payment each month. With the money you are making as profits, that still gives you a phenomenal return.

You can also ask the seller to finance the down payment, which means the seller will "carry the paper" as we discussed above. He will then be financing the entire down payment instead of just half. When you run the numbers, it still works great!

Worst case scenario, you could get a cash advance on your credit card or get a car title loan and use that for your down payment. Just make sure to pay the balance in full when it comes due. That should be no problem on a business earning $20,000 in profits before your small loan payments. That way you aren't paying any interest on your credit cards or other loan options, and letting that snowball, which would not be good for you or your business. So if you go this route, pay off that credit card or car title loan within a month or two – no ifs, ands or buts!

There are also websites on the internet that invest money to businesses, so you could also apply online for one of those for your down payment.

Or you could apply for a home equity line of credit on your house if you don't already have one in place. With your house as collateral, being able to qualify usually depends more on the equity you have in your home more than your credit score. $6,250 to $12,500 is a very small amount in the big picture. Just figure in the loan payments when you run the numbers to make sure you can afford it and that the business is still a good deal.

Also, if you have a 401k fund or some other type of retirement account that you can borrow against, that is also an option. If you pay it back within a certain legally specified time frame, you will only pay a small amount of interest but no IRS penalties. Talk to your CPA to make sure you are following the IRS rules to the letter to make this work.

Again, if you have selected a broker who has good financing connections, he should also be able to offer other possible suggestions or have his own connections for this very situation. So one way or another, there is *always* a way to make things work. If this is the way you want to go, don't give up until you find it!

Now, what if you are able to acquire your down payment, but your credit is marginal – too marginal for the SBA to give you a loan? Do you just give up? Not on your life! You *always* have options.

You can ask the seller to "carry the paper" and finance the entire loan (for 90% of the purchase price). Many sellers are agreeable to this arrangement, as it benefits them tax-wise. By taking payments over time, they don't have a great big capital gains tax bill to pay all at once. And with the savings in taxes, and a guaranteed 8% return on their money, they end up making much more on the sale because they get the purchase price from you *and* ten years of interest. All of which makes it very attractive to them to "carry the paper" on your purchase of their business.

However, if the seller is not willing to finance the loan for you, you still have the same options on the internet. Look under "hard money lenders" or "angel business loans." "Angels" are the nickname given to people who like to loan out money to new business owners to help them succeed while still getting a good return on their money. The interest rate may or may not be higher than the average of 8% that the SBA charges for interest rates. Just be sure to run the numbers and see if they still make sense before you go ahead.

Operating Expenses / Reserve Fund

Ok, so you've found the business you want to run, and have decided to purchase it ready-made from a business broker, and you have arranged all your financing and your down payment. Excellent progress! Now there is one more very important thing to consider – a reserve fund. Something used for operating expenses of your new business until the checks from your clients start coming in. I would recommend having $10,000 in your operating expense fund.

Invoicing Your Clients

Why do you need this $10,000 operating expense fund? Because here is the process for most service businesses on invoicing. If you are my clients for service for the month of May, here is how payment happens. I snail mail or email you an invoice on May 1st for service for the entire month of May, with the balance due on May 31st. Most of my customers would remit payment by May 15th. A few more would remit payment between the 20th – 30th of the month. And the remaining four or five clients would pay between the 10th – 15th of June for their May service.

For any one or two leftover clients that hadn't paid by the 15th of June, I would make a polite phone call to them, saying I'm *sure* it must be a clerical error on my end, but that my records show that I hadn't yet received payment from them. And then I would ask if they could please send me a copy of the cancelled check, front and back, so I could update my records to show that they had paid me. In this way, I wasn't calling my client a deadbeat, I was blaming myself, again giving my customer a way to save face for paying me late. Within a few days, I would *always* have my check in the mail. And by the way, this lesson in invoicing is how you should handle your invoicing for any service business.

But the point is, the money isn't pouring in the door from the moment you purchase the business. So depending on the date you close escrow, you could have four to six weeks of operating your new business without yet having any income coming in. So you'll need that $10,000 reserve fund to pay for your employees, and to cover any other additional operating expenses that may be needed. Once you get your first round of checks coming in, you'll be fine in all the coming months. But that first few weeks you will need some operating capital / reserve funds.

So where do you get this money? Again, from all the same places I suggested in order to get your down payment money. And again, repay this money as soon as humanly possible, so that you aren't drowning in debt. And before doing anything, make sure that the payments you will have to make to repay this money still fits comfortably in your business budget. *Always* run the numbers for *every* aspect of any business venture you decide to take on.

Due Your Due Diligence!

As you will see in a later chapter on "ready-made rental units" – units that come with a tenant already in them - there are definitely issues to avoid when buying a "ready-made service business."

Sometimes owners try to "cook the books," to make their business appear more profitable so they can sell it for a higher price. Never mind all their own printed documents, be sure to ask to see their business bank statements. Those will tell you the true picture about the business you are considering. You'll see exactly how much money is coming in every month, and how much is going out. Ask to also see the cancelled checks, so you can see if expenses are actually *true* expenses or just a shiny new sports car that the owner wanted to buy and "write off" as a business expense.

Also ask to see the contracts for the accounts they claim to have, and then verify those accounts. The way to do this without violating your NDA, is to call those accounts and tell them you are thinking of hiring the "Go Fly a Kite" Service Business. Tell them you were told that they are a client of the "Go Fly a Kite" Service Business, and that they listed them or their business as a reference, and you want to know how happy they are with their service. Do this for each and every account to verify their existence.

You can also ask to go along on the service routes "undercover" as a new "service trainee." This way, neither the other employees nor the clients will know you are a potential buyer. And it's another great way to verify that the accounts are real. You can also get a feel for the hired help and what type of job they are doing. And you can also discreetly pick the brains of the hired help to see if they might drop some useful piece of information that the owner "forgot" to tell you. Like perhaps the owner is about to lose three giant accounts in the next three months. If something like that is the case, the business could still be worth buying, but you would certainly need to adjust your purchase price accordingly.

You need to check out *every* aspect of this business in order to be sure you are getting the great deal you think you are. Also ask to speak to the CPA or bookkeeper for this business. If given written permission from the business owner, there should be no problem for the CPA to verify income and expenses with you.

The bottom line is you need to do your "due diligence" to protect yourself. Just like a house deal, you will have a certain time frame for due diligence, which means you can do all the research you want into this new business, and if it doesn't meet your expectations, you can back out of the deal and get your earnest money back, no problem. But you have to do it *before* the due diligence period runs out.

If the seller balks on any of your questions or requests for information, that's a big clue that something is wrong and you need to investigate further. But remember, until you have a signed contract to purchase the business and your earnest money deposit is in an escrow account, you don't have the legal right to be given this information.

Training Period

In all business sales, there is usually a "training period." During this time, the seller will teach you everything you need to know about the business. This will include introducing you to the clients and employees, show you the service routes and how the paperwork is handled, etc. Most training periods are from ten to thirty days. I would always write into the contract that you want the full thirty days. You may not need the full thirty days, and if you don't, that's fine. You can always tell the seller he is free to go early. But if you only allow for 10 days and you need a little more time, the seller has no obligation to help you. Always ask for the thirty days. Always protect yourself!

And congratulations – whether you decided to buy an existing business or were just finally able to discover the business that's right for you that you want to start from scratch, you are now well on your way to getting started. So now it's time to run the numbers if you have decided to start your business from scratch!

CHAPTER EIGHT

Running the Numbers

Now that you have a pretty good idea of the kind of business you want to start, you'll need to run some numbers on the costs involved in starting it. You'll want to know just how much money your new business is going to demand of you up front before you jump in.

But even before doing that, you should get some advice about what type of business entity to form. It's one thing to set up a card table and sell lemonade on the corner when you're eight. It's something else entirely to set up a business that's going to take in money, pay out expenditures, and fall under the watchful eye of local, state, and federal governments.

Your CPA is Your Friend – Really!

So first things first. What type of business structure are you going to set up? In my opinion - and this is only an opinion and not legal advice - most service businesses started out of the home are going to be *sole proprietorships*. They are generally the least costly and simplest way to go. I would definitely check with a CPA (Certified Public Accountant) and get his professional recommendation to be sure you are setting up the proper business entity. But most CPAs I've known over the years have told me to start with a sole proprietorship. Your CPA will advise you when or if you should ever change entities, based upon your own personal and financial circumstances.

     Your CPA will also explain to you what records you need to keep for your annual tax preparation. He will explain to you what are legitimate business deductions and what are not, and what documentation you will need to keep for these deductions. Generally, this is no more difficult than keeping a list of the income you received and the date you received it, as well as a list of the expenses you paid and the date you paid them. Your expense list should also contain a very brief notation for the reason for the expense. Also keep a milage log, which includes the date, the location that you traveled to, and the business reason why you went there, and the actual miles driven. The IRS allows a healthy deduction for business milage, which will save you on any income taxes owed.

     You want to be sure to take every legal deduction you are entitled to! Also be sure to keep your income and expense lists, your milage log, and all of your actual expense receipts in a handy file, in case you ever need them for an audit. As long as you maintain accurate, easy to access records to prove your expenses, and follow any other rules your CPA gives you, you'll have no problem sailing through any IRS audit with flying colors!

Licensed, Bonded and Insured!
     To find out how and where and what type of business license you will need, either look in your white pages of the phone book or do an internet search under "State of (name of your state here) Department of Business License." The white pages will give you a phone number to call for more information, and the internet will give you a government

website to go to that will show you all you need to know about getting a business license for your particular business.

The Department of Business Licenses for your state should also be able to advise you on where to find an "assumed name certificate" or a "fictitious name certificate." These are two names for the same thing. This form allows you to operate your business and open business bank accounts under your new business name, the "Go Fly a Kite Service Business" while signing checks with your personal name.

For almost every service business, you are likely to need only an "in-home occupancy" business license. Which as it states, means that you will be running the business out of your home. It usually comes with certain restrictions – you can't have customers or employees coming to your home, you can't have inventory delivered to your home. Basically, it allows you to run your home office through your home. And that's fine – on a service business, you are always going to your customer anyway. And if you ever do sell your customer a product (as in the case with my indoor plant business), you just have your wholesaler deliver the goods directly to the customers location.

And speaking of selling any products (as with my plant business), if you plan to sell any actual products (service is generally *not* considered a product) you'll also need to sign up with your state's "Department of Sales Taxation." You can find them the same way as you found the Department of Business License – phone book or online or even just ask while you are at the Department of Business License. You'll need to sign up for a sales tax identification number. Then on each sale you make for a product, you will collect the tax from the customer and usually turn it in monthly to the Department of Sales Taxation for your city and/or state. They will happily supply you with forms and instructions on how to do this properly.

You would also be wise to get a *bond* and *liability* insurance. Both are inexpensive, and both protect *you*. A bond protects you from theft claims from your clients against you or any of your helpers. Liability insurance protects you from any injuries caused to others by you or your workers. I was fortunate enough in all my years of conducting business never to have needed either one, but I would still advise you to get them, primarily for *your* protection. And they also look good in your advertising and promotional materials. Licensed, Bonded, and Insured has a nice ring to it, don't you think?

Initial Start Up Costs:
    Initial CPA Consultation: Should be free, to see if you are a good fit for each other.

    Business License: $50, depending upon the state in which you do business.

    Assumed Name / Fictitious Name Certificate: $2 for the form, $5 for a notary.

    Sole Proprietor Business Entity: $0. You just use your own social security number as your business tax identification number.

    Bonding: Approximately $50 for a bond that covers 10 or less employees.

    Liability Insurance: Approximately $300 a year for a policy with one million dollars of coverage. While you are your only employee, I'd buy the cheapest policy to start.

    Sales Tax Identification Number: Varies for each city and state, likely less than $100, could be free. And if you are not selling any taxable products, you won't need this at all.

Subtotal of Initial Start Up Costs:
    Worst Case Scenario: $507.
    Best Case Scenario: $207.

    These figures, I'm sure you'll admit, are pretty reasonable for getting a business going. However, they're not the only expenses you'll have to consider before being able to call yourself an entrepreneur.

Additional Start Up Costs:
Office Furniture

While some people worry about the cost of office furniture, I say forget about it. I never consider office furniture as part of a business start up cost. Wherever you live, you most likely have a table and at least one chair somewhere in your house. If for some reason you can't use the kitchen table to run your business in the beginning, spend $20 for a used card table, a folding chair and a small filing cabinet from a garage sale or thrift shop. There is no need to pay full price for these items at your nearest office supply store.

You can also ask your friends if they have any of these items lying around the house that you could borrow for your new business. It's likely they'll give them to you for free. But if not, simply return them once you begin making money and can buy replacements on your own. Total expenditures for office furniture: $20 maximum.

Computer / Office Supplies

What about a computer? That can be a pretty pricey investment. On the other hand, you most likely already own one that you could use for the limited amount of time that you'll need one in the early stages of growing your business. If you already have a computer, you're probably already "wired" to the internet, so there would be no additional expenses there.

In the unlikely event that you don't already own a computer and can't find anyone to let you use his, think twice before investing in one. You may find that you really don't need to spend anything more than $5 for an inexpensive calculator, a note pad and a pencil to keep track of your accounts, income, and expenses. And as a bonus, you won't ever have to worry about losing all your records due to a hard-disk crash or a computer virus meltdown! Remember – never invest money in something you don't actually need.

On the other hand, if you're convinced you must have a

computer to run your business efficiently and don't already have one, buy the least expensive one you can find – nothing over $300. Never mind all the bells and whistles - you can always add on later. What you need to worry about first is cost. And you can also get more bang for your buck at a local computer exchange that sells refurbished computer equipment for pennies on the dollar.

Promotional Materials

Of course, you'll also need to have some brochures, business cards and stationery made up. If you have a computer and are capable of doing a professional looking job yourself, fine. If you don't have a computer or don't know anything about layout and design, ask a talented friend with a computer to help you. You pay for the supplies (paper and ink) and in exchange offer to cook your friend dinner or offer to provide your services free of charge for a month. More expenses saved.

As an alternative, you can check with your local office supply stores or printing shops. They can often do the job quite professionally for relatively little money - perhaps $300 total for a thousand cards, brochures, and personalized stationery with matching envelopes. I suggest spending the most here that you can afford, since your cards and brochures are often the very first impression people will have of your new business. You want them to be impressed, informed, and comfortable in the knowledge that you can perform your service up to their expectations.

Advertising

Advertising is another potential expense, and for most service businesses, I would suggest placing a small, one-column-inch ad in the yellow page section of your phone book. That will cost you around $100 a month, depending on the part of the country you live in. Look at the ads your competition has placed, decide what features caught your eye, and borrow them for inclusion in your own ad.

You should also place several *free* ads on the various internet advertising lists available, as well as on all of the social networking sites online. You want to advertise in as many different ways as possible, as you won't know in the beginning which is the most effective for your new business.

Of course, you can save money by holding off on the yellow pages for a while and hand out brochures or business cards at networking events in your area instead. Check your local newspaper for networking events and go out and make friends *first*, and then you *will* make sales! You'll be your only employee for a while, and not likely to be swamped with customers at first, so you'll have plenty of time to attend these events yourself – and the cost is *free!*

Postage

Postage is yet another startup cost you'll have to bear. Buy a hundred stamp roll for around $50. Then send out letters to the biggest companies in your city, asking that they place you on their "bid list." You'll need to telephone them in advance to find out who their "decision maker" is for the service business you're starting, and ask what information they require in your letter to be placed on their bid list. Send that person a short, professionally written letter requesting to be placed on the company's bid list.

Many large companies accept bids only once a year. Be sure you find out when that time frame is so you don't miss any opportunities. The companies will send you their packages a month or so before the bids are due, laying out all of the requirements you'll need to fulfill in submitting your bid. It's critical to follow these requirements to the letter.

Transportation

Most people already own a vehicle of some kind, and if you do too, just use what you already have. No extra expense required, as your auto, gasoline and insurance are already normal monthly expenses in your personal life. No need to upgrade!

If you don't already have a car of any kind and need to make an appointment at a client's distant location, do what I would do. Take the bus or other public transportation, borrow a friend's car, take a taxi or rent a car for the day - and then try to schedule all of your appointments on that same day. The point is that until you have enough contracts to merit the purchase price of a car, do without. The price of a rental car is approximately $35 for a day. Or borrow a friend's vehicle for free, by trading your business service for a month or maybe a couple of hours of babysitting for their children.

So your additional start up costs shake out as follows:

Additional Start Up Costs:

Office Furniture: $20 at a garage sale, thrift shop, or *free* from a friend.

Computer / Office Supplies: $300 for a computer or *free* if you already have one or can use one that belongs to a friend. Or just $5 for a calculator, note pad, and pen if you don't need a computer.

Promotional Materials: $300 for brochures, business cards, company stationery and envelopes at an office supply company, or the cost of paper and ink (only $60?) if you can create your own layouts and designs.

Advertising: $100 or less a month for a one-inch yellow page ad. Zero if you feel a yellow page ad isn't appropriate to your business.

More Advertising: *Free* on the many internet classified advertising lists and social networking websites. *Free* to pass out brochures and business cards at networking events.

Postage: $50.

Transportation: *Free* if you already own a car or if you can borrow one when needed. $35 if you need to rent one once in a while.

Subtotal of Additional Start Up Costs:
    Worst Case Scenario: $805.
    Best Case Scenario: $150.

We'll talk in more detail about banking in a later chapter, but for start up cost purposes, let's take a look at banking, clothing and unanticipated expenses now.

Still More Start Up Costs:
Bank On It!
As far as banking goes, I suggest you find a local bank with a history of great customer service that offers the best deal for new businesses. That can mean free checks and no service fees so long as you maintain a minimum balance in your account.

Remember, once bank fees kick in, you could wind up paying $30 a month or more, which comes out to $360 a year *minimum*. Do you really want to give all that money to your banker? I don't!

One more piece of advice when opening your business checking account. Don't order the fancy checks that cost more. Instead take whatever checks the bank will give you free of charge. Remember, *free* is your new favorite price tag. *Cheap* is your next favorite word!

Dress for Success!
Clothing is also going to be a consideration to factor into your business start up costs. Remember, you get only one chance to make a great first impression. If you don't already have appropriate business attire, go to your local thrift shop or discount store and pick up whatever clothing is appropriate for the service you provide. You should be able to outfit yourself with at least six changes of clothing for about $50, possibly less.

If you're a girl, your ensemble may include one pair of business slacks, one pair of business shoes, one business skirt, and three business shirts in different colors so you can mix and match, plus a business jacket that is the same color as the slacks and skirt. Make sure all the items of apparel are in a color scheme that can be interchanged with one another. For example, the skirt, slacks and jacket all in black, brown or charcoal - conservative, serious business looking colors.

If you're a guy, buy two pair of slacks and skip the skirt. The rest of the list is the same as for the ladies, but throw in two or three neckties. It's likely that you'll meet the customer only once or twice all dressed up, once for the interview, and perhaps once again to sign contracts. And you'll also need your business attire available for your networking events as well. When you're actually performing your service, you'll need a nice pair of jeans and sneakers and a uniform shirt. You can have three shirts printed with your company logo, name, and telephone number so that you look like the professional you are while you're continually advertising as you work.

Remember to keep a handy dandy supply of business cards in your shirt pocket for potential customers. Have three shirts made at once so you don't have to do laundry every day. Go to your local t-shirt shop, where you can probably get the shirts for under $50 total. And if you don't already own at least one nice pair of jeans and sneakers, you don't live in America!

Unanticipated Expenses

That brings us to those devils of the business world, unanticipated expenses. For example, suppose a vital piece of your business equipment breaks down, such as a landscaper's one and only lawnmower. If your business is big and successful, you can afford to go out and buy a good quality replacement that will last for years. But if you're just starting out, I'd advise you to buy the cheapest one you can find through a garage sale, or buy from one of the many internet classified ad websites that list every conceivable item for sale. Or ask to borrow one from a friend in return for providing free service for his yard until you can afford to buy your own mower for *cash*.

As a last resort, you can also purchase a new mower from your local home improvement store. Some of the large home improvement chains offer credit cards to its business customers, so if you didn't have the money to pay cash up front, you *could* apply for that and pay off the balance as soon as the bill comes in. But make charges only when absolutely necessary and as your very last resort. Remember, debt is your enemy. Pay as you go whenever possible, since nothing will kill your business faster than debt!

Do you doubt me? Just look at our country and the recent recession - all caused by too much debt, which is simply a gamble with your future - a future no one can predict!

With that in mind, here are the results for these costs...

Still More Start Up Costs:
Banking: Approximately $30 a month or *free*.

Clothing: $110 or just $50 for the uniform shirts, if you already have the rest of your business wardrobe.

Unanticipated Expenses: $50 tops. Are you thinking these could actually be much higher than that? If you learn to think outside the box, you'll soon come to realize that you can solve virtually *any* unanticipated problem you encounter for $50 or less – maybe even for *free*. Where there's a will, there is *always* a way. Find it!

Subtotal of Still More Start Up Costs:
Worst Case Scenario: $190 - plus more each month if you run into regular monthly banking fees.
Best Case Scenario: $50.

Everything considered, then, after tallying up all of the start up figures for your new business, we find the costs in a worst case scenario to be $1,507. That isn't bad for going from no business ownership to new business ownership. Less than $1,600! Far less than most people would have anticipated before running the numbers.

But better still, is the tally of the costs in a best case scenario total, which boil down to $407 - less by far than $500! Do you begin to see some possibilities developing here? Are you starting to get a little excited? Can you picture yourself making this scenario work? Good.

Just remember when running the numbers to be as accurate as possible. Include every legitimate cost that you can think of. The more accurate you can be in identifying *all* of your business start up costs in advance, the more prepared you'll be. And the more prepared you are, the more successful you will be.

That doesn't mean you should panic if something unexpected pops up after you've started your business. After all, the words, *I will,* and *I can,* are now your mantra. The concept of *thinking outside of the box* is your new National Anthem. So what are you waiting for?

Just remember when running your business start up numbers - keep them low, low, *low.* If you can't do without it, borrow it or buy it used. That's the best equation I know for creating a new business that translates into win, win, *win!*

CHAPTER NINE

The Importance of Details

Starting a new business of your own is a little like doing anything from scratch. You first need to give the venture some thought, which you've already done while crunching the start up numbers. Then follow some basic rules. Anticipate having a few surprises along the way - and learning while you deal with them, of course! And be prepared to work a little harder in the beginning to get things up and running.

What should you do first after you've settled on the right business for you and you've run the numbers to your satisfaction? I thought you'd never ask! So I prepared a checklist, a step-by-step roadmap of the things I suggest you do to help get your new business moving. Starting with...

1. Structure. You've already decided upon the type of business entity that's best for you. That was one of the reasons you consulted with a good CPA rather than asking other people's advice, even from well-meaning friends and family members. The one time I took advice from someone other than a CPA, I structured one of my businesses in a way that would have cost me a *fortune* in taxes if I hadn't found a good CPA to straighten things out right away. I would have saved even *more* money if I'd hired the CPA first!

So let's assume a free initial consultation resulted in you locating a good CPA, someone you feel you can trust. If you don't know where to look for one, get recommendations from friends, neighbors and family members.

Next, set up a meeting for an interview. Ask the CPA about his fees and what his general recommendation is for your particular type of business - sole proprietorship, limited liability company, corporation, etc. Ask what he'd charge to set up your business structure for tax purposes. If his fee seems high, tell him so and let him know how much you *can* afford. A good, aggressive, *concerned* CPA may be willing to flex a bit on his fee schedule in order to help a new business venture get off the ground, especially if he knows you are looking to establish a long-term business relationship with him.

Follow up that meeting with interviews of other CPAs who might have been recommended to you. After talking with at least three or four, decide which one you're going to choose. I always prefer hiring people with whom I enjoy working. Life is hard enough as it is, so why make things even harder? If you select a CPA you enjoy spending time with, everything else will be that much easier.

A couple of additional points about selecting a CPA. Choose one with "Enrolled Agent" status. My own CPA is great. His fees are reasonable, and I can e-mail him questions all year long without worrying about his billing me for them. Just one bill for my tax return at the end of the year. My kind of guy - reasonable price, fun to work with, and you can't beat him for his qualifications and expertise. *And* he has a great sense of humor to boot! As you can imagine, I recommend him to *everyone* I know. Furthermore, I make sure he knows it.

Remember, a good CPA is worth his weight in gold. When your business venture gets successful enough, if you need to change your entity, your CPA can usually recommend a good tax attorney to set up any entity you require. And at that point, you'll have enough money to hire a good lawyer, and he'll be someone your CPA trusts and has worked with. But, just as in selecting a CPA you like, make sure the attorney you hire is similarly compatible with you.

2. Licensing. With government poking its nose into every aspect of our lives these days – like how much water you're allowed to use to flush a toilet, for example - it's likely that virtually *any* business you start will require some kind of license. I mentioned in the last chapter how to locate your local business license office.

But if you still can't find the right place to apply for your business license in either the white pages of your phone book or on the internet, check with your competition when *you are interviewing them*, as I advised in Chapter 4. Ask them if they're licensed and if so, with whom, because you prefer doing business with licensed contractors. Ask to see a copy of their business license. Then write down the contact information of the business license office. No reputable business owner would ever be offended by such a request, and most will gladly provide you with the answers to your questions.

3. Bonding. Next you will want to get bonded. Again, this protects you and your employees from any accusations of theft from your customers. This is done through a commercial insurance agency. If you don't know where to find a commercial insurance agency, you can ask your regular insurance agent for the name of one that he trusts. Or you can look one up in the yellow pages or on the internet.

4. Commercial Liability Insurance. You will buy this policy from the same commercial insurance agent that sold you the bond for your business. Then, if any of your clients gets injured due to an accident caused by you or your workers, and the client wants someone to sue, they'll be suing the insurance company instead of *you*.

In the beginning, when you're still your only employee, I recommend acquiring the least costly bonding and/or liability insurance you can find, since it's highly unlikely *you* will ever cause anyone any situations due to theft or carelessness resulting in physical injury. But it gives your customers peace of mind, knowing that you take your business, and your customers' well-being, seriously. And most importantly of all, you protect *yourself* and *your business* by being bonded and insured.

5. Registration. As with licensing, registration is required in order for you to conduct banking business under your business name. This is why you need to get an "Assumed Name Certificate" or a "Fictitious Name Certificate." Again, check with the Licensing Bureau in your area or do an internet search to find out where to get the proper form to be filled out in your state. Your family banker can also usually give you the information you need to locate this form in your state. We'll have another chapter later that goes into more detail on banking and the importance of selecting the right bank for you and your new business.

6. Naming Your Business. What do you name your new business? Now is the time to do it, before you set up your business entity and before you apply for a Business License, Bonding, Liability Insurance, or an Assumed Name Certificate, because you'll need your business name on all that other paperwork. Here are some thoughts that might prove useful.

Think two words. Short and snappy. Also a name that generates some type of familiarity is best. The name should convey a feeling that you want associated with the business. For example, my pet-sitting business was called "Pet Pals." Again, short, easy to remember, and has a warm fuzzy feeling about it, since it's caring for someone's family member - a pet.

I recommend taking a look in the yellow pages at your competitors' names. See if any "buzzwords" in the industry jump out at you. Then just brainstorm. Write down every business name you can think of, no matter how stupid or silly or crazy it may seem. Then set the list aside for a few days. If anything else pops into your head in the meantime, add it to the list, but don't review your previous offerings just yet.

After several days have passed, look at your list. You'll know immediately which names are just awful, so don't hesitate to cross them off. You'll likely end up with four or five survivors. Play with them. Say them out loud. Are they awkward sounding? Or do they give you that excited feeling again, the feeling that tells you that you are on the right track? Maybe this one is the winner?

Try saying the following phrase, as if you are answering your phone: "Thank you for calling (potential business name), this is (your first name), how may I help you?" If it doesn't roll off your tongue easily, forget it. If you need to, set the list down for a couple more days. Your brain will continue to "percolate" all the while. When you next review your list a few days down the line, you'll just *know* in your gut which is the right name for you. It will be the business name you like most.

One other tip - don't get held up on ego on this one. Your own name on the business does *not* add credibility or value to the business and might actually work against you, because at this point in your business life, no one knows who you are and won't care. It's a rooky mistake. So long as your name is on the checking account, that should satisfy your ego. You want your business name to leave a great first impression, and part of that impression is to look professional while conveying a good feeling about what your business is to your customers.

7. Funding. Since we've already determined that your new business venture should cost you between $500 and $1,600 to start, let's just take the average and say you will only need $1,000 to get going. It's possible you already have that lying around in cash in a savings account. If you don't, most people I know have a credit card with at least a $1,000 limit. As long as you buy the items you need and then pay it off immediately upon receipt of the bill, you won't get yourself in trouble. But if you can't afford to pay it in full, I wouldn't recommend the credit card route.

So my next suggestion would be to get a part-time job to come up with your seed money. It won't take you long to save up $1,000 from a part-time job, and the part-time job itself will get you in the habit of spending those extra hours working, which you'll soon be doing on your new business venture anyway. And you never know if you might make a contact at your part-time job that will be in need of your new business services! Win-win!

Also, depending on the type of business you start, you may have most of the items you already need around the house - a big savings there! And with computers and desktop printing, you may even be able to make your own brochures and print your own business cards, so even more savings!

If that's not the case, don't worry. I'm virtually computer illiterate, so I make my own rough designs and then take them to my local office supply chain to have them turn out the final brochures and cards for me.

My point in funding your new business is this. It doesn't take a fortune to get things rolling. If you have good credit, a credit card, or a few dollars in the bank, you're ready to rock-and-roll!

And, speaking of banks, do *not* take out a loan to fund your new business until you read the following chapter, which is all about banks and banking.

8. Defining Your Services and Pricing. This is important so as not to have any misunderstandings or worse - legal repercussions for what your customer perceives to be false or misleading claims on your behalf.

For *whatever* service business you choose, you'll need to have a contract prepared that spells out *exactly* what you'll be providing as your standard service in exchange for X amount of dollars. For example, in a landscape business, it's standard to mow, blow, bag up the debris, check and repair all sprinkler heads regularly, and re-program sprinkler timers as the seasons and watering requirements change. A landscape service also weeds and trims all shrubs and bushes on a regular basis.

Your price would naturally depend on the size of the property, as well as on how high-maintenance it is. Mowing grass is more time-consuming than taking care of trees and a few bushes surrounded by mulch or rocks. More mowing takes more time, costs more money in gasoline and man hours, and causes wear and tear on mechanical equipment, all of which will cost you more time and money.

In setting your fees, your bid to each customer will be different based on the size of the job and any machinery involved. But the services included will basically be the same.

Be sure to include everything you need in your legal contract. There are many websites that offer legal contracts for very low prices, depending on what type of contract you require. Or, if you don't have enough money to buy a contract, when you are interviewing your competition (as recommended in Chapter 4), tell them that you *want* to sign up for their service, but you have to have a copy of their service contract for your spouse to review before you can sign, because he/she handles all of the household finances and "legal mumbo jumbo." *Voila!* You now have a *free* contract to work from that has most likely already been double-checked and okayed by an attorney.

Rewrite that contract with your own business information and any legal changes you need to make for it to better suit your needs. Then show it to your lawyer for his final seal of approval.

There are many things that you (as a non-lawyer) wouldn't even think of putting in your contract. Things that are basically "boilerplate protections" for you and your company. By having a lawyer review your contract, you'll avoid unpleasant situations in the future. You don't want to get sued for something that you could have avoided, if you'd only had the standard protections in your contract.

9. About Attorneys

Most lawyers will give you a free consultation, just like

a CPA, to see if you are suited for each other. That's also the attorney's chance to win you over as a new client. And it's your opportunity to feel out the attorney about your situation and his qualifications, to see if he is a good fit for you and your business needs. If all else is equal, choose the attorney you enjoy working with the most at the best price you can find. Just like the CPA, let your potential attorney candidates know that you are looking to establish a long-term business relationship, and that if they can be flexible on their fees in the beginning (before you are making any money) that you will come back to them for all your future legal needs, as well as recommending them to all your friends.

Also, see if you get the feeling that your potential attorney cares about *you* and *your company's* needs, instead of simply trying to make some fast cash off of you. You should expect your "vendors" (your CPA, your attorney, your bankers, your temp agencies, etc.) to give you the same feeling of security and confidence that you'll want to provide for your customers.

One word of caution about contracts. "Verbal" is *never* good enough. Remember, a verbal agreement is only as good as the paper it's written on - and it's not written on anything! Furthermore, verbal agreements are not usually binding in most states and under most conditions. Even if they *are* legal in your state, how are you going to *prove* the provisions of the agreement in a court of law should a dispute arise? You *don't* want to start your new business getting bogged down in a he-said/she-said legal battle that ends up costing you money. Contracts need to be written in order to protect *you*. Always!

10. Marketing and Promotion. Depending on the service business you start up, a small yellow page ad may be enough to get the word out. On my plant and pet businesses, I started with a very small 1-column-inch ad for each, which cost me $100 a piece each month. And I also made sure to get on the bid lists for the big corporations for my plant business. I chose to go the yellow page ad route because I thought it was most suitable for those two businesses.

And I don't love cold calling, even though I did it very successfully for my lingerie business. I also wasn't too keen on networking to hand out brochures or business cards, even though I had done a lot of that for my nightclub, and the fliers did generate *lots* of customers for that business. I'm sure I could have grown both my plant and pet businesses much more quickly if I had done some cold calling and networking for them as well. But I just didn't want to. And because I was the boss, I didn't *have* to!

I like to joke that "I'm not ambitious, I'm lazy." I just sat on my fanny and waited for the phone to ring for my plant and pet businesses. And I still managed to retire at age 38. If I hadn't disliked cold calling or networking so much, imagine how much faster I could have retired! Or with even more money! But that wasn't my personality. By working only 2 - 4 hours a day no more than four days a week, I considered myself to have been semi-retired by the time I turned 20.

As my plant business grew, I eventually got a much bigger ad (about the size of 3" x 2.5") which got me many more calls. By the time I sold that business, my "little" ad was the largest and classiest in the yellow pages, and I was raking in the dough. So if you're gregarious and love cold calling, do that. If not, do what I did and take out an ad.

And of course now there are free classified ad websites all over the internet, as well as many social media and professional media networking websites. I say try them all and see what works – especially since they are free, it's not costing you any extra money. I do recommend tracking your advertising. As new customers call in, always politely ask them how they heard of your company. Keep records, and you'll soon see a pattern of where your advertising and marketing time, effort and dollars bring you the greatest return. Once you see that pattern, focus the bulk of your advertising and marketing on those venues.

The bottom line is that you can promote and market your new business without spending thousands of dollars on television and radio commercials and full-page newspaper ads. You can do it for little-to-nothing, and you can succeed!

11. Performance. This isn't even up for debate, is it? Remember this simple work ethic: *Whatever* you promise to do, *do it!* And whenever possible, especially on your first go-round with a new client, do a *little bit extra,* and before you leave, show your new client what you did that was "above and beyond." But don't charge anything extra. That shows your client in a humble, "I care about you" sort of way that you're devoted to your customer and not to scrounging more money. Impress your customer, and he'll shout your praises to everyone who will listen. The word of mouth will spread like wildfire and the referral business will come pouring in!

Another aspect of performance: Offer your client a 10% discount from his service fee for that month for any new customer he sends you. Win-win situation. Just don't forget to deduct that 10% off your next invoice whenever your clients *do* send you a new customer, or you'll only alienate them and cast doubt upon your own good word.

Remember: *Always* keep your word. Do what you promise, and do it without exception. *Always!*

12. Warranties. From my business owner's point-of-view (and remember this is *not* a legal opinion), a warranty is *not* something in your favor. I would stay away from warranties in general. Don't put them in your contract, and don't mention them in your promotional material. It's possible that you can have performed your service *perfectly,* but every once in a while, you'll come across "*I Want To Make Everyone Miserable*" for a client, and if you give him a warranty, you could easily end up in court trying to *prove* that you lived up to it. Even though you *know* you did. So, no warranties - not in my opinion. But again, check with an attorney if you have any doubts.

Remember, it's always been my philosophy that *my* contract, written for, paid for, and dedicated to protecting *me,* should do just that. *Not* protect my customer. As much as we want to keep our customers happy, you can't please everyone. So protect yourself first and foremost. In all the years I've been in business, I've never *once* been sued by a client. Part of the reason for that, I'm convinced, is that I set out to do a good job (better than advertised, in fact) *without* offering a warranty of my services.

Do a good job, have a happy client. And, as word gets around, you won't *need* a written warranty.

13. Welcome to The Club! One of the seemingly small, but actually *very* important, things you can do after obtaining a new client is to reach out and let him know you appreciate his business, which is the same as letting him know you appreciate his faith in you. That's why I recommend writing him an introductory "welcome-to-the-club" letter that goes something like the following letter. Tailor it to suit whatever your particular service business is, of course.

> Dear Mr. and Mrs. John Smith and Rover,
>
> I just want to let you know how pleased we are to welcome you as a new client in our pet-sitting family. We look forward to many happy years of caring for Rover while you're working or on vacation.
>
> For your records, here is our office telephone number for scheduling. Or you can contact me on my cell phone at any time of night or day by calling 000-5555.
>
> We have also enclosed a box of "Welcome to our pet-sitting family" cookies for you and your family, plus a box of doggie biscuits for Rover - naturally!
>
> Thank you again for your business! We appreciate it greatly and look forward to earning your trust.
>
> Sincerely,
> Aimee Elizabeth

Then whenever you dog-sit Rover, the day before Mr. and Mrs. Smith come home, make sure you have plenty of inexpensive stationery with your company logo and business name on it, and leave a little note, saying something like this:

Dear Mr. and Mrs. Smith,

Welcome home from your trip! Rover and I hope you had as much fun as we did. On Tuesday we played ball for an hour (he does love to fetch!). Then on Wednesday I scratched his belly and he fell asleep all snuggled up to me, so we had a nice nap together. On our walk on Thursday, he saw some neighborhood doggie friends and they wagged tails to say hello. We had a wonderful time together, but I know how happy he'll be to see you when you get home.

Thank you again for your business! And for allowing me to share Rover with you, for however shortly!

Sincerely,
Aimee Elizabeth

    This "new client thank you letter" formula can be applied to virtually *all* businesses. Although I recommend sending it only once for anything other than the pet-sitting or any type of child-care or business - people like to feel like they know what their babies (animal or actual) were up to while they were gone. For all other businesses, the initial "new client welcome letter" is a nice touch that will go a long way toward creating good will and a long-term business relationship. After that, a simple yearly holiday card, thanking them for their continued business, perhaps with a little $5 gift card for the local coffee house chain stuffed inside, will help cement relations.
    Just a little something to show you care - about the *person*, and not only the business. That's something to remember always.

CHAPTER TEN

Banking On a Winner

You'll need to open a checking account for your new business. Pick the right bank to handle your finances, and it can be a blessing. Pick the wrong one, and you may regret it.

For a new business owner, there is a big advantage to using a local community "mom and pop" bank. The people who work there want to get to know their customers, and that means *you*! Their primary focus is on customer service, and they tend to go the extra mile to help you succeed.

Choose to do business at a large nationally franchised bank, on the other hand, and you may be sorry. Some large national banks provide excellent customer service, but others provide as little customer service as possible. Check around with friends and family to see who recommends what bank to you. Whether you choose a large or small bank, the most important criteria for choosing your bank is excellent customer service, a desire to help you succeed, and a willingness to go above and beyond the call of duty.

Just as with your choice of CPA and attorney, you need to interview your potential banking candidates to see if they are a good fit for you, *before* you decide where to bank. And just like all your other business relationships, you want to deal with people who you enjoy working with.

At a community bank, you tend to develop a nice friendly business relationship with the tellers and managers because they tend to have a low turnover. You see the same people every week when you make your deposits. So you chat a little every week and make friends. Then later on down the road if you ever need a loan, your personal relationship can push the decision in your favor.

At large nationwide banks, however, they tend to have a high turnover in their staff. So it's sometimes harder to develop that nice friendly business relationship that can be so helpful, because every couple of months the tellers and managers seem to change. That can make for a very impersonal business relationship, since no one ever really gets to know you. And since no one really knows you very well at a large national bank, if you ever did need a loan, it's likely they would only consider your credit score and that's it. They wouldn't be trying to go the extra mile to help you because they don't know you personally.

And for anyone with a credit score that's just "on the edge" of your bank's loan requirements, a personal relationship with your banker can make all the difference on getting a loan approved if you ever need one. We are going to hope and plan that you don't ever need a loan for your new service business, but it's always best to be prepared, just in case. And when it's time to finance your first rental property, there is a small chance that you may want to finance it through your bank, so it's good to keep that option open as well.

Credit unions are also like community banks - they *want* to help you, *want* you to succeed, *want* to have a relationship with you. They genuinely *care* about their customers, and it shows. And that's why in general, I recommend smaller banks and credit unions for all your business and personal banking.

Online Banking

I know that a lot of people these days like to use their computers to make purchases, sell things online, and even bank online. I've never used online banking in my life, and I probably never will. Besides, as with large national banks, online banking is far too impersonal for me. I want my tellers and bank managers to know me, so if there's ever an unusual situation, they'll want to help me out because they *like* me.

"Make a friend, make a sale" is a critically important part of my business philosophy. That applies to your vendors as well as to your customers. Sure, the vendors are there to serve you. But in today's environment of *zero* customer service, if you treat your bankers kindly and make a point to spend a few moments asking about their kids or complimenting her beautiful bracelet or his attractive tie, they'll go out of their way to help you when you need them.

Treat your vendors the way you treat your customers - always be happy, always be pleasant, always be courteous and thankful for their help. Tell them you don't know what you would have done without them. Treat them well every single time you interact with them, and they'll remember because *no one* gets compliments these days. Stand out from the crowd, be sincere, and they'll *want* to go that extra mile for you.

Drive-Through vs. Personal Banking

Drive-through banking is just one step above on-line banking. And it's still too impersonal for me.

Personal banking is definitely the way to go, but face-to-face, not through the fast-food lane! Make yourself a fixture at your bank. Go inside often. Along with asking about your bankers families, share with them in a low key way your future business plans or how business is going in general. But no bragging! You want your bankers to like you, not to think of you as an arrogant jerk. Help them get to know you, who you are, and what you've done in the past, and they'll be rooting for your success.

Another good piece of advice - never express impatience if you have to wait in line. If other people in line complain loudly, tell them even more loudly how you think these are the best bankers in the world, and that they're obviously doing the best they can possibly do at such a busy time of day. The bankers will hear you and appreciate your loyalty. Better still, they'll want to reciprocate. Be sure to mention when you get to the front of the line what an "creep that guy was" and bemoan the fact that no one has good manners anymore and everyone is so rude. And when the time comes for making that business loan or helping you solve an unusual situation, your bankers will be jumping through hoops to help you.

Finding the Right Bank

Of course, finding the right bank for you can be a bit daunting. Not wanting to waste time and money driving all over town, I usually pick a small community bank closest to home. Once I open an account, I ask them what the minimum amount is that I have to keep on deposit in order to have zero service fees and unlimited free checks. I open the account with that minimum or more, and I make sure that I never fall below it.

If you're new in town or unfamiliar with the banks near you, you might check the yellow pages to find the closest ones and look them up on the internet to see what they offer for new business accounts. Or simply telephone them and ask.

You could also drive to each bank, explain to someone in the office what you hope to accomplish, and sit back to listen to the spiel. If you get a heavy sigh and a lot of attitude, I wouldn't bank there if they paid me. But if they seem excited, as if they're anxious to help you and they have experience with your type of project, that could be a sign that you've just found the bank of your dreams, even if the fees are a little bit higher than those of the competition.

This is one place where you don't want to be penny wise and dollar foolish, especially not if your goal is to get a loan one day. From my point of view, I dislike owing money. Because debt can make you a slave and if used improperly, it can be a *huge* liability to your business and your life. That's why I prefer to pay cash as I go. But there are always exceptions to every rule, and there are definitely times when borrowing money can be advantageous for your particular situation. So it's always good to keep your options open.

If you're sure you're never going to need a loan, choose the bank nearest to you with the most services for the least amount of outlay. Besides, your ultimate goal is going to be to get into real estate where you likely won't be borrowing money from a bank, but rather from a mortgage broker.

Banking On a Good Deal

One of the nice things about opening a new bank account is all of the freebies you can get for yourself - *if* you've selected the right bank. Free checking, free online Bill Pay, free checks for life, sometimes even access to your own personal banker - you could qualify for many of these services if you maintain a high enough minimum balance in your account- usually $2,000 or $3,000 - or if you just happen to time things when your new bank is offering a big promotion to bring in more customers.

Regardless, having a couple-thousand-dollar cushion in your account is a very nice thing indeed, so I recommend you always try to maintain more than the required minimum.

To Borrow or Not to Borrow

What if you have no credit cards, no credit or, worse still, *bad* credit? Isn't that reason enough to try to get a bank loan to fund your new business?

Well, with no credit or bad credit, no bank is going to lend you money anyway. So forget about that. Pick yourself up, dust yourself off, and start all over again.

Go out and get a part-time job to supplement your full-time work. Once you have enough saved up for the start up costs for your business, then you can quit that part-time job and get started! It won't take long to save up the little amount of money it will take to start your new service business.

Do you see why that Winner Mentality is *so* important?

There's *always* a way to become a success, but only if you're committed to succeed.

Maintaining Financial Diligence

While you're at it, make sure you don't fall prey to what I call the "Swelled Head Mentality." That's what happened to the partner I had in my nightclub. He began thinking, "I own a business. I'm my own boss. I call the shots. I'm going to be rich. I can buy anything I want now." That's a *loser's* attitude. You have to maintain low overhead and watch the pennies and dollars like a proverbial hawk - both in business and in your personal life. Just because you're doing well - better, perhaps, than you'd ever thought possible - doesn't mean you can take a break from the one who brought you here.

Maintain financial diligence. It takes some self-discipline, but it pays off *big time* down the road. Over and over again.

If you can change your attitude about money as I have advised you here, you'll change your life - for the better - both financially and personally. And that's just exactly what I *want* you to do!

CHAPTER ELEVEN

Work Smart, Not Hard

Now that you have your first business up and running, you're going to start thinking about growing it. How to make it larger, more profitable, and more fun!

You might think that the pursuit of more business is a difficult or at least tricky affair. It can be, but it doesn't have to be.

For any meeting with a potential client, whether you have a scheduled appointment or you are cold calling, you will *always* want to focus on the benefits to the client.

For example, the lingerie shows provided a way to consistently increase food and beverage sales every week in the lounge on the nights we worked. More revenue generated in the lounge made the manager look like a hero to his boss.

For another example, a benefit of the plant care business is healthier air that living plants provide inside of airtight office buildings – plants provide more oxygen for people to breathe in, so there are less sick days taken by employees. They also give a peaceful, happy feeling to employees, so employees are more productive. All benefits to the business owner.

On the pet business, the benefits to the family is they have peace of mind knowing their pets, plants and house are all safely cared for while they are away. The benefits to Rover or Kitty are a familiar person to come and give them love and attention while their family is gone, so they don't stress out from separation anxiety. All benefits to your clients – human and animal!

See how this works? Make a list of all the benefits that *your* new service business will provide to your clients, and focus on those benefits at your sales presentation meetings. If you focus on the benefits to your potential clients, they will see the value of your service, and they will be begging to sign up for your service!

And as a general rule, I advise never talking about money until the client asks about the price. Talking money first simply shows the customer that you care only about getting your hands on his cash, which will only alienate him.

Closing the Deal

By this point, after showing your potential customer all the benefits of your service plan, he is likely very interested and will ask the price, your signal that he's ready to sign on the dotted line. If your customer never does get around to asking the price, you'll need to step in and close the deal. Remember that 95 percent of all deals fail to get put together for one reason only - *you fail to ask for the order!* The customer expects you to close the deal. He takes it as a lack of conviction on your part if you don't.

Here are some examples of closing questions...

What date would be most convenient for us to begin your new service plan? Notice this is not a *yes* or *no* question. You are assuming the customer is already agreeable, and you merely need the details. *How often would you like your service performed? Daily, weekly, bi-weekly, monthly?* If for some reason the customer balks, as a last resort you can always suggest a trial period. *Let's do a trial service plan for one month. If you don't agree that we're great for you and/or your business, don't hire us back.* Remind him, however, that if he does agree that you're worth every penny, you'll continue your service on a regular basis.

Cold Calling / Sales Presentation / Follow Up Tips

If your potential client already has another company performing the service you are offering, I'd ask if they were happy with their current company. If there was any hesitation, I'd try to snare their business.

One point to remember - never talk bad about your competition. All that does is make you look unprofessional, and no one will want to hire you.

If they're happy with their current arrangement, tell them how glad you are to hear it. Also tell them that you're always available to perform a comparable service at a more reasonable price. Never say "cheaper," which can be misinterpreted to mean *less valuable service.* They may be agreeable to that. If not, be polite, thank them for their time, and let them know if they're ever looking to change services in the future to give you a call. Leave your business card and marketing materials behind.

Also, check back in six months to see if they are still happy with their current service and to see if there may be a new manager in charge. New managers have to justify their existence by making changes, and that could include giving your company a chance to increase their business.

Also, take notes on your current and potential clients. Are they married? Have kids? Hobbies? Then, each time you visit, check your notes and be sure to ask the manager how is your wife, Marie? And Sam, your son - is he ready for college yet? And are you still flying model airplanes on weekends?

All this continues to show you *care* about your customers - and makes them delighted to see you, even if they're only *potential* customers. One tiny piece of negative feedback about that "other company" they're using could bring these guys running to you, because they see you as someone who is qualified and really *cares* about them and their professional needs. That same display of personal interest will keep these people loyal to you when something goes wrong. They'll give you a chance to fix any issues, all because you took the time to develop a real *relationship* with them.

What's the Best Way to Promote *Your* New Business?
Of course, the role you play all depends on your personality. I have done cold calling, fliers, networking, yellow page ads and getting on the bid lists of large companies. I have to admit, I prefer kicking back and just letting the phone ring. I like to know I'm wanted before I go to an appointment. If that's your personality too, then get into a service business that most people select from the yellow pages. If you're super aggressive and a real go-getter, then it doesn't really matter. You can do all of the above yourself. But in the beginning, until you're making lots of money and have developed a feel for which type of advertising is best for your particular business, I would try all of these options.

How Much Time Should You Devote to Promote?
Until you have customers, there's no reason *not* to work as many hours a day as you can. If you have a full-time job to work around, then perhaps you'll be able to work your business one or two hours a day, three days a week. Or maybe 8 hours a day on the weekends. If you don't have a full-time job, then you should be able to promote eight hours a day until you have customers taking up your time. And if you are marketing eight hours a day, you'll soon have lots of customers!

There's no hard and fast rule here. As your business begins to sprout and then grow, you'll have less time to do the advertising and promotional work yourself, at least until you hire someone to cover your first route, after which you'll have plenty of time again to promote - see how that works?

Is Any Job Too Small?
In my case, I found the smallest accounts were the

easiest to pick up, since "the big boys" service providers didn't want to be bothered with those "small fry" accounts. So I gave great service to the small accounts, and you know what? When their businesses grew, I was their established service provider already, so they just stuck with me. Suddenly, several $60 a month accounts grew into $600 a month accounts *overnight* because my clients had expanded their businesses and my services then required more time (meaning more money to me). The clients never even asked other companies to bid because "the big boys" had looked down their noses at these small accounts way back when, so I could pretty well "set my own price" for the additional service fee - although I was still always fair. But suddenly 5 small accounts at $60 a month each were now earning me $3,000 a month in total – with no extra salesmanship on my part. What a great feeling *that* was!

The larger accounts are harder to get, but once you land a "whale," or your small fry accounts grow into whales, they give your company a whole new level of credibility, because for some of those corporate "bid packages" I mentioned, you'll need references from three other large accounts.

Is a Yellow Page Ad Right for *Your* Service Business?

One way to find out is to ask yourself this question: *If I was going to hire this type of service business, how would I look for one?* If your answer is to check the yellow pages first, then that may be just what you need. Another way is to check the yellow page ads for your type of business. Do they even have a category for your business? If yes, that's a pretty big clue that the yellow pages may be a huge help to you.

In the beginning, buy only the cheapest ad you can comfortably afford, and make it as classy as possible, using buzzwords and catch phrases from other ads that made you view them favorably. Then track your sales and see how many customers each month are generated from that ad.

And *always* include the following language someplace in your ad - "*Best Possible Service, Lowest Possible Price.*" Also, make sure your ad is clear, concise, and *uncluttered.* Take it out for the shortest period of time possible – generally six months to a year is the normal initial contract term for a yellow page ad. That way, if you find the ad isn't pulling its weight, you can stop paying after your contract period is up. But if it gets you even two customers a month, it's likely worth it.

Breaking Down Your Time

I'd suggest spending 40 percent of your marketing time cold calling by phone or in person. If you are calling by phone, here's a great time to call those referrals given to you by friends and family (which I'll be discussing shortly). If you go unannounced and in person, be sure to stop at the dollar store and by a tasty sweet treat for the decision maker's secretary or executive assistant – that person is the "gate keeper" for the decision maker. Get on her good side, and she might happily persuade her boss to grant you entrée into his decision making kingdom. Get on her bad side, and you can guarantee that the decision maker won't even know you exist.

Then use 30 percent of your time networking and passing out brochures, business cards and fliers, trying to drum up both new business and referrals. Look in your daily newspaper, there are many networking functions every week that you can attend. You may meet someone who needs your services or you may meet someone who *knows* someone who needs your services and can refer you! Just remember to focus on making friends first, before trying to cram your business card down someone's throat. People enjoy doing business with other people who are friends. But treat these potential clients like a slick used car salesman would, caring only about closing the sale, and you'll alienate potential customers.

Then spend the remaining 30 percent of your time getting on the bid lists of the "Bigs," and arranging your yellow page ad (if appropriate) as well as your free internet classified ads and social networks. Once you've set up your free ads on the various internet advertising lists and networking websites, and have arranged for your yellow page ad, those won't require any further time or attention. The same goes for the "Bigs" – once you are on their annual bid lists, there isn't much more to do there until they send you out the annual bid packages.

So what should you do with the time you had budgeted to the "Bigs" and setting up your advertising? Hopefully by now, you will be filling that leftover 30 percent of your time to service your new clients!

Whenever new potential customers call *you*, make sure you ask them, "How did you hear about us, if you don't mind my asking?" And keep a log of the responses. That's an excellent way to determine where to sink the bulk of your advertising and promotional time, energy and money in the future.

After a few months, you'll begin to see a pattern emerge, and you'll know which form of advertising works best for your business. Then concentrate most (but not all) of your efforts on whatever is working best. I would still always keep a toe in the water of any and all of the marketing avenues that generate even a little business for you – because you never know which marketing avenue may lead you to a whale. And you don't want to risk missing out on them! And I would still *always* remain on the bid lists for the big companies (the whales), even if they're not paying off right away. It only takes *one* Mr. Big to turn your business life around.

To give you some real life examples, my first huge client in my plant business came from my yellow page ad. Another giant came from being on the bid lists. Other enormous accounts came from referrals from the first huge client (the one from the yellow pages). Another massive account came from a dance partner friend of mine who was a high ranking decision maker in his company. And several of my "small fry" accounts grew into whales after a couple of years. You just never know where your next big account will come from. Which is why you want to keep as many avenues open as possible for your marketing and promotion.

Practice Makes Purchase...

You should also make a list of *all* your friends and family. I assume they would want to help you succeed. Then ask them if you can "practice" your sales presentation on them - with no obligation to buy anything, of course - in order to help you sharpen your marketing skills. If they like your presentation and have a few questions, answer them honestly and openly, and certainly allow them to sign up for service if they want to. But remember to honor your promise to them – no obligation to buy, so don't pressure them, they are helping you practice your presentation. They might also have some helpful suggestions to make your presentation more successful. Whatever their reaction, be gracious and thankful that they are trying to help you.

If they do *want to* sign up, give them a first-month-free "family discount" if they sign up for a one year contract. Whether or not they sign up for your service, let them know that you would *really* appreciate them giving you the contact information on the decision makers at their place of employment so that you can make an appointment to pitch your services in a discreet, low-key way. Offer to give them a 10% referral fee off the first month of service for any of their referrals that sign up - a great incentive for everyone involved!

Also ask if they would suggest to their friends that they give you an opportunity to prepare a bid for them. Keep up the word-of-mouth bids and proposals, and offer those who agree to help promote your business a 10% referral fee on the first month's service from any new accounts generated by their referral.

Once you receive a potential client's name from a friend or relative, call their office and say, "Hi, my name is (your first name), with (name of your service business), and (name of your friend or relative) in your office suggested I give you a call to schedule an appointment to show you our service plan. What would be a good day and time for me to stop by for just five or ten minutes to show you how I can provide you with the *best* possible service at the *lowest* possible price?" Again, just as with a "closing question," this is *not* a yes or no question. This is a question that assumes the potential client is agreeable to meeting with you, and you just need the scheduling details for the meeting. If you ask *yes* or *no* questions, you make it way too easy for your potential client to say no. And that's not your goal. This is a "soft sell" way of getting what you want, while offering the potential client something he also wants – the best possible service at the lowest possible price!

It's always good to have a connection, so don't be afraid to ask permission to use it. And be sure to let them know you won't be hard-selling anyone they refer you to either. That's just not your style.

Make a Friend, Make a Sale!

One other word on "hard selling" - this can often get you an immediate sale, but it *always* leaves a bitter taste in the customer's mouth, although he might not really know why. Even if you do your job perfectly, he'll eventually replace you at the first opportunity, because that bad "hard-sell" taste will always linger.

Instead, practice "soft selling" - which is what I call "make a friend, make a sale." Show the potential customer that you care about *him* - by asking how his wife, Marie is doing? And how is his son, Sam, doing in college? Or did he catch the latest model airplane show in town?

Also, in your sales presentation, always explain all the ways that your company will benefit *him and/or his company.* That's "soft selling." Not only will your customers be happier, but *so will you*, because you'll both have a happy, pleasant, friendly working relationship.

A "hard seller" is basically a bully. And even if the customer *needs* your service, even if you provide better service at a more affordable price, *no one* likes to play with a bully.

Remember, "hard sellers" (like used car salesmen) are not in it for the long haul, and every customer in the world knows it. Well, *nearly* every customer! Hard sellers want that immediate commission *now* and don't care if they ever see you again.

"Soft sellers" on the other hand, are viewed as friends, and friends are treated with loyalty and respect, which of course you give in return, and the happy business relationship lasts for years to come. Your customers are delighted to give you referrals, talk you up to everyone, and endorse you simply because you make them feel good. "Make a friend, make a sale." It's truly the key to success. All the rest is just logistics and math and occasional problems to be solved.

Handling Problems Properly

Of course, *everyone* knows that unpleasant situations come up in every aspect of life. It's just the way it is. It's how you deal with those issues that can make or break your business. For example:

A customer calls up yelling at you, claiming that your employee made some type of mistake. Maybe it's a legitimate complaint, and maybe it's not. Perhaps the customer was recently yelled at by *his* boss and wanted to yell at someone, *anyone*, else. And you won the lottery that day!

So, here's how you handle *any* and *all* complaints, regardless of whether your company messed up or not. "Yes, Mr. Wonderful Customer, I am *so very sorry* this happened. I accept *full responsibility* for this mistake. I will drop everything and be down at your company *today*, so that I *personally* can correct this problem, and also show my employees the proper way to do this in the future. And as a way to make up for your inconvenience, I'm going to reduce your next month's bill by 20%."

Let me tell you what happens next. First, all of the anger disappears from the customer. No one in today's environment of *zero* customer service *ever* says, "I'm sorry." No one *ever* accepts responsibility. All anyone ever does is make excuses.

Likewise, no one *ever* comes by *today* to fix the problem. Especially not the *owner* of the company. And no other company *ever* reduces money on the next bill. *Every single time* I had this conversation, here was the response I got from the customer:

1. The anger instantly vanished.

2. He felt sheepish for yelling at me.

3. He thanked me profusely for my great attitude and my willingness to drop everything to make the situation right (showing the customer how important he is to me).

4. Even more surprisingly, my customers absolutely refused to allow me to deduct 20 percent from their next bill. Let me repeat that - not one of my customers *ever* would allow me to reduce their next bill. Obviously, the way I responded to the complaint gained for me even more loyalty and trust because of my sympathetic handling of the situation. I handled it properly, and I cemented the business relationship for years to come.

5. As a bonus toward further cementing your relationship, once you have fixed the problem, stop by the customer's office to show him *how* you fixed it so that he knows you lived up to your word, knows that *you* actually rectified the situation yourself. Then shake his hand and say, "Great to see you again, and how is your wife, Marie? And how is Sam's college major in journalism going? And did you see that recent model airplane show?"

6. Also, remember to *thank your customer* for bringing the problem to your attention, because you never wanted to provide any less than the best possible service to him. Let your customer know that he has done you a *favor* by alerting you to the problem. Make the customer feel good about himself, and he'll feel good about supporting you and recommending you to others.

Remember, it's *always* more expensive to find a new customer than it is to keep an old one satisfied. Treasure every customer you have, always treat them like gold, and soon you'll be sitting on a *pile* of gold yourself. And before long, you'll never have to work another day in your life. And isn't that our goal here?

Never Enough, Never Enough!

Someone once asked me, "When do you know that you've taken on enough new business?" My response is simple. There's no such thing. There's *never* enough new business. Ever. If all that new business seems overwhelming at first, "I will" and "I can" will see you through.

Of course, that's not a problem you're likely to have early in your entrepreneurial career. In the beginning, there will be no work, so it will be almost impossible to overextend yourself. All you'll be doing then is trying to drum up business and survive. Once you get some business, stop drumming and get to work until that work is done. Then go back to drumming up more business. But let's pretend that you have reached the point where you now have four days of work each week for your new business, leaving you with only one day a week for your marketing. And now suddenly you land a whale that's going to create four more full days of work each week for you. What do you do?

You call a temporary employment agency. They supply all types of skilled and unskilled labor to all kinds of different businesses. Check the yellow pages and call around to find the lowest prices.

For manual labor (which most service businesses are), you'll likely be paying around $10 - $12 an hour for each helper, and the temp agency pays all their taxes, insurance, benefits, etc. That keeps you clean with the IRS, without having to deal with "employees" of your own. So now overnight you suddenly have eight days of service that needs to be performed in a five-day work week. For this example, we're assuming that the service is unable to be performed on weekends or nights - only your basic eight-to-five weekday-type schedule, although situations will vary from company to company, so rearrange my advice to suit your needs.

You call the temp agency, and you tell them you need to hire one person to work with you four days a week, from 8 a.m. - 5 p.m., doing "X" type of labor. And now with two of you working, the work goes twice as fast. Plus you're right next to your new temp, training and supervising him as you go. Now you get eight days of work performed in four days, because you have a helper. And if your helper is good, you keep him on as a "full time temp." If he's not good, you keep calling the agency until they send you the right guy, and that one you keep.

Voila, you now have performed as promised for all your clients without overextending yourself. And you landed your first "whale" in the process while doubling your income - nice job!!!

Once you find the right temp for this route, and he's been properly trained, I'd break out into two routes. Give him five full days and keep three yourself. Now you have two days available for marketing again. And when you get your fourth day full, or land another whale, call the temp agency again and train your next helper. There are *lots* of people who work as full-time, permanent temps. Temp agencies supply their employees with health and unemployment insurance, vacation time, and pay the employers share of any taxes due - none of which you'll need to worry about.

Bottom line - there is *no way* to overextend yourself. You're safely covered. Let's say you land three "whales" at once that require four days of service each. And wouldn't *that* be a great day? Now you simply hire three temps to go with you. You work whale #1 with all three guys on the first day. You do whale #2 with all three guys on the second day. You do whale #3 with all three guys on the third day.

Then you take all three to finish up the rest of your accounts on the next day or two. No problem. Again, stay with your new helpers until you see that they are qualified to do the routes themselves, and then just assign them to that one giant account to work on their own. And while you're busy training your new guys to handle the whales, you drop your marketing for a couple of weeks. And there is no problem on dropping your marketing for a couple of weeks, since you basically just quadrupled your income!

Or, if you already have guy #1 trained from your first big whale, send him around to train your new helpers, while they help him on his big account on the first day. But I find for all accounts, not just the whales, that it really helps to go the extra mile and do the work yourself the first few times, just to make sure it's all done properly and you have made that great first impression. New clients really *love* to see that the owner isn't afraid to get his hands dirty to make sure it's all done right. And it's important, also, that the guy you send in your place later understands clearly what's expected of him.

How Tough on Hired Help?

I believe that all expectations you have of your hired help should be very clearly explained to them from day one. Let them know that as you work alongside them during the training period, you will be correcting them as needed until you see they have the proper hang of things, at which point you'll turn them loose on their own to work unsupervised. Remind them that you know how many hours each job takes, and you won't be paying for more than that, so lollygagging isn't going to benefit them.

And while you may say to one of your workers, "Hey, Derek, will you please hand me that pencil?" It's critical that they understand you're *not* asking them a question. They have no choice in the matter. You were merely being polite while giving them a direct order, and the only correct response is "Here you go, boss" as Derek hands it over.

Keep in mind that you're the dictator and your workers are your subjects. You can give the orders politely, but they are orders nonetheless and must be complied with promptly and completely. When Queen Elizabeth says to her handmaiden, "Will you hand me my tiara?" you can bet your sweet bippy she's not asking a question - she's giving an order, cloaked in politeness. Queenie understands that and so does her maid. You need to make certain from *day one* that your help understands, as well.

And while you're at it, you might as well cover some other critical ground rules:

1. Make it clear that there's no "hitting on" clients or their employees or friends. Your hired help should be polite and cordial, but also businesslike and hard working. Their job is to finish the work and get out of the way of your customers.

2. Resist the temptation to become friends with your employees, or they'll only take advantage of you. Trust me on this - it's important. Don't engage in pleasantries or small talk with them, because that's a waste of time and money and sends your help the wrong message.

3. Make your help prove their value to you always, and don't let them bother you with things *they're* supposed to be doing.

4. Never *ever* give an employee an advance on pay. That's not how things are done in business, and this is *your* business. Once you start providing advances on pay, your workers will come to rely upon them - and upon you being the perennial "sucker."

5. Make it clear that you will not tolerate slacking off or frequent sick-day call-ins. This isn't a developing friendship. It's business, pure and simple.

Remember, there's nothing ruthless about being typically businesslike. After all, this is *your* business, remember? Are you going to allow your hired help tell you how to run it? Not on your watch! And *no exceptions!* If your help doesn't like the rules, let them find work elsewhere.
That doesn't mean you should curse them out or humiliate them or treat them poorly. As an employer, I like to think that I'm hard but fair. I fully expect my hired help to commit to doing their jobs. "I will" and "I can" applies to *them,* as well as to me. I don't want a whiner, I want a winner! Think of the parent/child relationship - it's my job to babysit and train them until they can be independent on their own. And it's my job to correct their behavior along the way.
I will occasionally compliment them on a job well done, but not always. Studies have shown that rats who are only

sporadically rewarded with cheese when they push the right button will push it much more regularly than a rat who gets rewarded all the time. The same applies to gamblers and, of course, to workers. Sincere compliments on occasion are good, but only sporadically.

Also I tell my help up front that I have a system, and I don't deviate from it, *ever*. End of story. Deviating from your system wastes your time, and wasting your time *always* costs you money.

Hard but fair - that's what you're after with your hired help. You do what you promised to do for me (the work, done promptly and properly), and I do what I promised for you (I pay you on payday).

If you simply can't find it within you to be a stern taskmaster, then the best course of action is to pretend that you're only the business *manager* and not the *owner*. Explain to your workers that while you'd like to bend the rules, the owner is a ruthless tyrant who would fire you in a heartbeat the very first time you did. It's a little variation on the "good cop/bad cop" game that works quite effectively. You still get to be the "good cop" while enforcing the rules of the "bad cop." Everyone who works for you still likes you, but they understand they simply must follow the rules, just like you do, to protect their jobs as well as yours.

How Much Help is Too Much?

If you stick to hiring full-time "temps," there is no problem with the IRS. And temporary agencies are fine with that, since they make money off everyone who works for you. Plus the agency continues to pay for the temps' taxes, unemployment insurance, vacation pay, etc. You deduct your bill from the agency as a business expense, no complications, and you're home free. There are no restrictions on your business growing too big to handle. So long as you and your CPA report your earnings honestly, and you pay whatever taxes you owe, the IRS will be ecstatic that you're succeeding and expanding, since that means they'll receive more money from you.

And speaking of Uncle Sam, please always remember, it's not worth fudging figures with the IRS. Whatever amount of money you are taking in, take all of the legal deductions your CPA says you're entitled to, then pay the required taxes on your profits and you're free to enjoy the fruits of your labor. Try to dodge the IRS, on the other hand, and you'll live in constant stress and fear, and who wants that?

Keep in mind, it's always better to have a tax problem than a cash-flow problem. If you have a tax problem, it means you're making tons of money - and that's terrific! You should have plenty of money left over to pay some of it to the IRS.

To Compete or Not To Compete?

There are a couple more things you need to know before hiring temporary help when growing your business. By working with a temp agency, you'll never have any legal pitfalls because you're not hiring or firing anyone - the agency is. *They're* on the hook for all the paperwork, withholding tax, workers comp and unemployment insurance, etc. If one temp doesn't work out, you simply call the agency and say, "This guy isn't working. Can you send me someone else?" and they will.

What an agency *won't* do for you is get you a non-compete agreement. You'll have to do that yourself by having every one of your temps sign before you even show them their first job. A "non-compete" prohibits your temps from stealing your customers from you. It makes your customer list a trade secret and protects your proprietary business secrets from use by unauthorized persons.

By the time you've gotten your temps to sign the non-compete agreement, you'll be well on your way to becoming a seasoned temporary help employer. You'll find, as I did, that hiring temps from an agency is the absolute best way of hiring help. It's much quicker, easier, and more effective than running an ad in the local paper, or hanging a "help wanted" sign around your neck!

So, find an agency that works well for you, befriend the agent that seems to be the most "client-centered," and treat that agent like gold. Just as you do with everyone you meet.

You'll reap the rewards of that relationship a thousand times over, and that's something you can take with you to the bank!

CHAPTER TWELVE

I Quit! **How to Know When the Time is Right**

Okay. Your business is up and running. You're making money. Perhaps you're expanding by taking on a temp worker or two. But you're still working your full-time job. Is it time to quit? And, if so, how can you tell? And if you're wrong, won't you be committing financial *hari-kari?*
There are actually several things to take into consideration before making the plunge into full-time self-employment. Here are some of the more important ones.

Analyze Your Situation
Here's a look at the formula I suggest for determining just when you should begin thinking seriously about quitting your day job - and, more importantly, when *not* to:

1. Don't quit your full-time job until your business is earning twice your monthly expenses - including the cost of health-care insurance, as explained in number three, below. If you wait to quit your day job until that point, you won't feel the financial pinch so much if you lose an account here or there. No big deal. You'll still have a financial cushion.

2. Don't quit your day job until you have at least a six month safety net of personal expenses saved up. If your expenses are a thousand dollars a month, you should have six thousand in an account. If they're two thousand a month, you should have twelve thousand. If your expenses are five thousand a month, then you should have thirty thousand in savings. That way if business slows down, you're not in an immediate bind. You'll have at least six months of "cushion" in order to figure out a way to build your business revenues back up again.

3. Don't quit your full-time job - and lose your benefits - unless you have a spouse or domestic partner who can add your name to his or her health insurance policy. If you don't have a spouse or domestic partner who can add your name to his or her health insurance policy, then prior to quitting your regular job, you'll need to call a commercial insurance agent. I'd recommend calling the same one you purchased your bond and business liability insurance from. Then ask for a quote on a "major medical" policy with a $10 thousand deductible. A deductible that large will make your monthly rates *much* more affordable than a $500 or $1,000 deductible. But that's just fine, because you don't need to run to the doctor or the E.R. every time you get a minor cut or come down with the sniffles. What you want to concern yourself with are potentially life-threatening illnesses that can drain your savings overnight.

Don't Skimp on Insurance

By the way, it's absolutely necessary to have health insurance (at least the catastrophic kind), since you don't want to build up a fabulous nest egg destined to turn into your early retirement fund only to have a major health issue wipe you out. Don't be penny wise and dollar foolish here. You want to keep what you've worked so hard to get and grab that early retirement, which will last you for the rest of your life - *if* you plan properly. You don't want to have to go back to work after a debilitating illness has bankrupted you financially and destroyed your good health.

I retired at the age of 38, fully expecting to live forever - or at least until the ripe old age of 100 if science hasn't figured out how to clone me by then! And I *know* I'll always have enough income to live on. In fact, my net worth rises significantly each year, so I stay well ahead of the inflation curve and never have to live in fear of my money running out. Which is exactly the same state of economic freedom that I want you to be enjoying shortly!

Still not convinced of the value of health insurance? Here's a short story that will change your mind.

My second ex-husband, who despite our divorce is a very nice guy, had no health insurance when we married, but neither did he have any apparent health issues. He had assets and so did I. So I told him he needed to purchase major medical insurance, and he balked and bullied me and resisted doing so. I told him, "Listen, if you have a heart attack (which is what I genuinely feared would happen since he was already overweight, never exercised, and ate enormous steaks for dinner each night), they'll take all our assets to pay your hospital bills. Only poor people get free medical treatment. They'll take everything we own, do you understand?"

He looked at me and said, "So if I have a heart attack, just shoot me."

He's a nice guy, as I said, but not the most practical in the world. So I told him, "Great plan! I'll shoot you. You'll be dead. Then I'll go to jail for the rest of my life. And there won't be anyone left to care for your 90-year-old mom. You know, the one you promised never to put in a nursing home?"

Well, I finally got through to him with that, and he reluctantly agreed to buy a major medical insurance policy. It cost him just a little more than $200 a month with only a $5,000 deductible. It even paid for most of his doctor's office visits and prescriptions, with just a minor co-pay, much to our pleasant surprise!

A couple of years after buying the policy, he developed rectal cancer. The only reason he's alive today and he wasn't financially devastated by the cost of his treatment is because I insisted he get insurance while we were married. My ex was the type to *never, ever* go to a doctor. You couldn't drag him to see a physician if you held a gun to his head! But the insurance company required he get a physical before they would issue the policy. That policy revealed high cholesterol and high blood pressure, and in order to get the policy he had to remain under a doctors care to treat and monitor his blood pressure and cholesterol on a regular basis. In fact, after he got his blood pressure and cholesterol back down to healthy levels, I applied for a reduction in his insurance premiums, and they were granted, so then he was paying a little less than $200 a month for his premiums. But he still remained under that doctor's regular care for his medications. When my ex-husband turned 60, that same doctor ordered a colonoscopy, and that's when they found the rectal cancer. It was stage 2, almost stage 3. He was extremely lucky, as it hadn't yet spread anywhere – but it was about to!

Today, he's fully recovered with little prospect of a recurrence. I tell him to this day that he owes me his life, because if that cancer had continued to grow inside of him for another year and spread throughout his body, (since he would never have voluntarily gone to a doctor), he'd be dead today.

Despite the fact that he argued with me over *everything* throughout our marriage, he wholeheartedly agrees that he *does* owe me his life. And if he ever gets snippy with me, you can bet your boots I remind him of the fact!

Lifetime Cap on Coverage

Another thing on the major medical insurance issue. My ex-husband's medical bills totaled in excess of $500,000 to treat his cancer. But he only ended paying approximately $10,000 out of pocket. The cancer could have killed him or wiped him out financially or both. But that major medical policy turned a potential catastrophe into just a minor blip –

both medically and financially. So be sure to be insured!

One final note on medical insurance. Medical costs have sky-rocketed as everyone knows. $500,000 may sound like an enormous amount of money to cover my ex's cancer treatment. And it's certainly a lot of money. But there are other diseases, illness and injuries that cost even more to treat than just $500,000. Most major medical policies have a lifetime cap of a certain amount of money. That means that if your cap is at 2 Million, and your bills run up to 2 Million, you are now out of coverage on that policy. Finished, kaput, done.

And if you have ever had an illness that cost you that kind of money, believe me, no one else will insure you once you run out of coverage. So make sure your policy has a lifetime cap of *at least* 2 Million dollars. 5 Million is preferable, but it may be out of your price range when you are just starting out. Purchase the least expensive policy that has the highest lifetime cap for coverage. Later on when you can afford it, go back and upgrade to the 5 Million dollar lifetime cap. You'll be glad you did later if anything happens to your health.

Some Pitfalls to Avoid

So let's assume you've handled the insurance issue, you have six months of living expenses in the bank, and your business is generating twice your monthly expenses. You're all ready to quit your day (or night) job. You've planned and hoped and schemed and dreamed of this day forever. But suddenly, you're not really sure if you can bear to leave your friends and co-workers behind. Could it be?

Most people don't realize it, but most adult friendships revolve around common interests more than the length of time you've known one another. Inside the workplace, that common interest is work. Once the common bond of working together no longer exists, most co-worker friendships tend to die a natural death. It's nothing personal. You just move in different circles, different directions, until finally the friendship feels more like work than fun. So you drift apart.

Count on it. That doesn't mean you don't still have fond

memories or that you won't e-mail one another occasionally or get together for lunch - at least for a while. But unless there was more of a bond between you than the workplace, the relationships will fade over time.

Now, if one of your co-worker friends also shared a common leisure activity with you - perhaps you both like to go camping on weekends or enjoyed playing tennis or doing an aerobics class together - those friendships will continue, because they didn't revolve totally around work. But you generally won't be *as* close as you were before because you won't see each other every day anymore.

A friendship based on proximity (work), rather than on commonalities (shared leisure-time interests), is going to fade. Accept it.

Also, get used to the fact that, once you move into self-employment full-time, you won't be making friends with your new workers or your new clients. There's a reason for the phrase, "It's lonely at the top." Once you set out on your own, you can't befriend your staff any more than you can your clients. Doing so only messes up the entire friendly business relationship that you want to have with these people - friendly but without being friends.

It's a fine line to walk, because once you cross that line, the expectations of your staff and your clients will change. The employees will expect special treatment because they view you not only as a boss, but also as a friend. You'll lose control of that employee, and your "friend" will begin infringing upon your life and your privacy when all you wanted to do was to keep him as a pleasant worker or client at arm's length.

If you're still concerned about the loss of your personal contacts at your day job, I'd recommend keeping that job until your business has grown to the point where you can't possibly expand further unless you quit. By that time, exhaustion will kill you anyway, so you might as well sever the ties!

If you're concerned about being lonely, make sure that you have a core group of friends outside the workplace with whom you can socialize in your off hours. If you don't already have that separate group of friends, I suggest signing up for some classes in things that interest you so you can make new friends away from your job. Sign up for a photography class, if that interests you. Or a dance class - a great way to socialize, exercise, and meet new friends of both sexes. Join a bowling league one night of the week or a pool league or a gym. Whatever interests you in your leisure time, sign up so that you can make new friends based on common interests.

It's not easy to break away from the group. Humans are social by nature and tend to pack together like dogs for safety. But you bought this book, you want to be special, you want to retire early and enjoy life instead of being a hamster running that treadmill everyday of your life. So you have to take my advice.

When you quit your day job, you will eventually lose most of your office friendships. It's not the end of the world. Replace them with new friends based upon your common interests. And remember, you can never tell in advance which of your old or new friends might turn out to be a new customer or maybe even a whale!

Making the Split Easier
Many people may think they have an office full of friends from years of working closely together. Sure, you have a bond with them - it's the work. But if you don't have much else in common, once you leave, you'll simply drift apart.

Don't feel badly. It's just that once you leave, the bond is gone. It's a similar with men going off to war. Their close proximity to one another creates a bond for life, and they're always happy to see one another on occasion. But they don't usually hang out together after the war is over.

It's the same with most jobs. They, too, are a battlefield of sorts - the employees pitted against management or whoever the office lunatic is - and so you bond. Once the war is over (you no longer work there), you're no longer in the same army with these people.

When you leave, some office friends may even be jealous that you're trying to better yourself. Because they don't have the courage to do so themselves, they may try to discourage, disparage, and even disrespect you. Some will show outright signs of scorn or disdain. Others will cry when you leave because they'll miss you so badly - you added so much joy to their lives.

But it's all part of life, a fluid, unpredictable thing. You will be surprised at who will be proud of you and cheering you on, and you'll be shocked at who acts as if you're betraying your friendship. Remember that the naysayers are jealous because they don't have the courage to try for the brass ring themselves. And if you try and fail, they'll feel better about their own miserable little lives. And those miserable lives will still contain a very limited amount of income potential - whereas your income potential is unlimited once you become self-employed!

Their lot will remain unchanged. They'll still have to battle management and corporate stupidity and co-workers they can't stand every working day of their lives. You, on the other hand, will be master of your own fate. If you don't like how a worker performs, you just call the temp agency, tell them your current worker isn't working out and tell them why, and they will send you someone even more suitable for the work. You don't even need to tell the unsatisfactory worker that his time with you is over. That's the job of the temp agency, who will just tell that worker that the job with you has ended, and they will place him on another job. No awkward or unpleasant confrontations for you. You never even have to fire anyone when you are using temps – the temp agency even does *that* for you!

So, remember that people who exhibit a sour grapes attitude toward your success are doing so only because you've achieved the freedom they wanted but couldn't get - financial freedom, freedom to use your time as you wish, freedom to earn as much money as you want, freedom to do work that you *love*, freedom to work with the people of your choice and to work with the clients you choose. You even have the option not to work at all and hire a manager to run your business!

You have the freedom to take vacations when and where you want, without having to ask permission for days off so long as you have a reliable crew lined up to take your place.

Justifying Your Departure

Of course, when the big day comes and you announce to one and all that you're going to be quitting, the first question you'll hear is, "Why?"

Keep your response humble and modest - you always want to maintain happy relationships, even when those relationships are ending or changing. You never know when a former employee will turn into a paying customer. Always remember - *Make a Friend, Make a Sale*.

Tell your coworkers (if they don't already know) that you started the "Go Fly a Kite" service business a few months ago, just to make a little extra pocket change and because you love flying kites, making custom order kites, and teaching others how to fly kites. Much to your pleasant surprise, the business boomed! Now, you're doing so well that you simply can't handle both your new business and your job anymore. Tell them you're going to miss them, but you had to make a choice, even though doing so was difficult. But, since you so love the "Go Fly a Kite" service business so much, you feel compelled to follow your bliss.

I wouldn't emphasize how much money you're making - it might lead to someone hitting you up for a loan. Instead, say that the business isn't making you rich, but it *is* making you happy. People are less jealous of happiness than money. Don't ask me why!

So give everyone your new business card with your contact information so that they can stay in touch with you. And, of course, possibly be a source of new business for you, although I wouldn't tell them that! Some people may ask about the details of your business, and you should answer them honestly, since you may walk out with a new customer or two in your corner. But don't try actively selling on your way out the door, because that can create the feeling that you were merely using your workplace buddies.

If someone should happen to mention that they have a relative who would like to learn how to fly kites, on the other hand, be upbeat: "Wow, that's terrific. I love referrals. And if your cousin calls and signs up for a class, I'll send you a 10% commission from that class. In fact, I'll do the same for any new clients you send me. Just be sure to have your cousin mention your name when he calls, so I know to send you that commission check."

Now you've got your ex-co-workers sending you business. And you've just given them a small piece of credit, of recognition, of validation, by letting them know how much you appreciate their help in helping you to succeed. When you give people credit, most resentment vanishes. When you invest others in your success, they'll want to keep helping you so that they can continue to look good and feel good - and, of course, collect those commission checks! It's a win-win situation, which are always the best kind.

Telling the Boss

This might seem a bit trickier, telling the boss that you're going to be leaving shortly. After all, but for him, you wouldn't have had a job in the first place.

So he deserves your honesty. He's going to hear the truth through the grapevine anyway, and he deserves to hear it from you first, before you tell your co-workers. Be respectful by giving your two-week notice, or whatever company policy demands. Use the same humble and modest speech you plan to give your co-workers. So long as you are humble, gracious, courteous, and respectful, your boss can't help but take the news well. If he's a good person, he'll wish you the best. If he shows interest in your business and future plans, offer to send him a commission for any referrals you sign up.

Also, be sure to tell your boss how much you have enjoyed working for him, how fair and accessible you always found him to be, and how much you've learned from him - whether or not it's true. Mention that, except for his mentoring, you doubt you could have opened your own business. Always share the credit for your success with others. People love having their egos stroked, and by letting him know how grateful you are for his training, he becomes invested in helping you to succeed. After all, didn't you just tell him you couldn't have done it without him? Likely he'll be the one organizing your going away party - or at least ordering his secretary to do it! Besides, you never know when your old boss will go to work for a new company just aching for your services.

Always Remember: The two biggest keys to success in business are *"I Will"* and *"I Can,"* and *"Make a Friend, Make a Sale."* Success in business is all about your commitment to success and relationships - making your customers feel good. Since every person you meet is a potential customer, you should always do your best to bond with everyone you meet. It doesn't cost you anything, and it might just gain you a paying customer one day!

CHAPTER THIRTEEN

Finding Your First Rental Property

After you've severed your ties with your former employer in order to devote more time to building your own business (instead of toiling away at building his!), it's time to begin thinking about where to find that first rental property you're going to want to acquire.
But what kind of rental? After all, there are all kinds of investment properties on the market. The following paragraphs will give you my recommended criteria, as well as my reasons for my criteria. If you understand why, you'll be much more likely to stick to a winning formula!

Rental House Criteria – A Recipe for Success!
It's really quite easy. You want to buy a three bedroom, two bath, single-story house *not* within an HOA (Home Owner Association). Those are the criteria I can give you for buying rental property. Oh, yes, and right around 1,300 sq. ft., with

low-maintenance landscaping (lots of rocks, gravel, and low-water plants). And the building should be no more than 10 - 15 years old, preferably *near* HOA properties - so you still have the cachet of advertising in the "fancy part of town" - but never *in* an HOA. (More on why *not* to buy into an HOA later in this chapter).

Also, make sure that whatever property you settle on is either in "move-in ready" condition or that it only needs some cosmetic work. Cosmetic work includes cleaning or replacing carpeting, touching up or re-painting the entire unit, maybe some landscape clean up, trash removal, some cleaning, and some minor repairs that a basic handyman can handle. Nothing complicated, nothing too expensive. These type of repairs can be done quickly and cheaply. And time is money when you are sitting with an empty rental unit being prepared for your renters to move in. All of this cosmetic work can be done in about a week's time or less, and for not much money. And you can get your first renters installed before your first mortgage payment is due, which is the goal. Usually that first mortgage payment is due approximately 45 days *after* your close of escrow.

Stay Away from Broken Houses!

What you *don't* want is a house where someone converted the garage into a spare room. You *don't* want a house where every appliance, including the air conditioning and heating units and all the wiring, have been ripped out of the walls and ceilings. You *don't* want a house where the owner did a very bad job at installing permanent add-on rooms, or permanent but poorly installed cabinets. You *don't* want a house where there was ever mold damage. Have your insurance agent run a *CLUE report* for you on the house during your due diligence period. It will tell you if there was ever a claim for water or mold damage on the house. It's sometimes difficult or impossible to sell a house that ever had an insurance claim for water or mold damage. And it can be equally difficult to purchase homeowner insurance on such a house.

Also have a home inspection done on the house. While it may cost you approximately $300, it will usually reveal any problems you may have missed, and then you can negotiate with the seller to pay for those repairs, so your home inspection pays for itself and then some 99% of the time. And in this case, an ounce of prevention really is worth a pound of cure. Better to spend $300 to learn you don't want to buy a "broken house" than to blindly buy the house for $100,000 and live to regret it down the line.

While we are planning for you to hold your rentals for a long time, you always want to be able to sell them if something in your life changes. It's always best to keep *all* your options open. When I see houses with these kinds of damages, I say that the prior owner "broke the house" and I want nothing to do with it. I am interested in doing some simple, easy and cheap repairs for cosmetic damage only. I am not looking to re-model or worse, re-build a house before it's ready for a renter. That can take way too much time and money (possibly several months and tens of thousands of dollars), and while all that money is going out for repairs, your house is sitting vacant for quite some time while all this heavy duty re-model and re-building is going on.

So just say no to broken houses!

Still More Criteria for Your Rental Success!

Also, buy close to good schools, shopping, public transportation lines, and good freeway access. All these things are great selling points for your tenants. And buy in a neighborhood where at least *most* of the houses have good curb appeal - with no junker cars in the front yard, no dead couches as lawn furniture, and no peeling paint on the front porch. You want to buy something you would be willing to live in yourself. After all, if times ever get tough, you may someday have to do just that!

Buy the smallest house in the nicest neighborhood, since the bigger homes will bring the price of your tiny property up. On the other hand, if you buy the biggest house in that neighborhood, the tiny houses will bring your property values down.

Just Say "No" to Stairs!

You also want to buy a single-story home because stairs add risk - someone could fall down the stairs and sue you. Of course, you'll be insured against that by your homeowners insurance policy, but if a suit happens, your insurance company will either raise your rates or possibly non-renew your policy – even when they prevail in your defense! So it's best to hold liability to a minimum to avoid that possibility.

Also, stairs cost more to you as the owner but they don't increase your monthly rents and they actually *detract* from the value of your investment property. Why? Because stairs add square footage, but they don't add usable space for your tenants, but most home prices are based on square footage, so you end up paying more right off the bat to *buy* the house with stairs. Then you also end up paying more for property taxes and homeowners insurance, since those expenses are based on the purchase price for the property taxes and the square footage for your homeowners insurance. So more money out the window for no good reason.

Worse yet, when it's time to clean or replace the carpet, you have to do the stairs, so again, you are paying to maintain or replace non-usable square footage for your tenants that generates no additional rent for you. And cleaning or re-carpeting stairs is more labor intensive than just cleaning or replacing carpet on a flat floor area, so you are paying more labor costs for your cleaning and re-carpeting as well.

Also, some very desirable tenants have health issues that prevent them from being able to climb stairs. You don't want to miss out on those tenants! Especially because tenants with health issues generally *hate* to move, because their health issues make it virtually impossible for them to do all the heavy lifting needed to move. And due to the extra costs of a health issue, they likely won't have the money or the energy to want to move. A nice, reliable tenant with a health issue will happily rent your single story home for years to come if you treat them right on maintenance and rents.

And if you ever decide to sell your property, a single story will usually sell for a premium when compared to two-story homes. All good reasons to stick to single story homes, for you *and* your tenants!

Why buy a place with low-maintenance landscaping? Because tenants won't care for your lawn even if they're required by the rental contract to do so. So avoid large areas of grass, and opt instead for lots of trees, bushes, and inorganic ground cover - gravel, stone, or wood chips.

Buy the Right House, Attract the Best Tenants!

Why buy a 1,300 square foot home, with three bedrooms and two baths? Because families move into 3 bedroom homes, and families are who you want as renters. Families want to "put down roots" and become friends with their neighbors. As their children make friends in school and in your neighborhood, they won't want to leave, ever. You will have long-term tenants if you rent to families.

Single men and women, however, don't make a good bet for long-term tenants. If they suddenly get into a serious relationship, then they may want to move in with their significant other, get married and buy a house, or they may decide to accept a job transfer to another part of the country. Single people are much more transient than families. Also, roommate situations are even worse than a single person. What if the roommates don't get along and one moves out? Or what if one of the roommates gets married or accepts a job transfer or moves in with a significant other? If the remaining roommate can't afford your place without a roommate, now you have lost rents after they either leave voluntarily or you waste even more time and money going through the eviction process.

Now, I'm not advocating any type of discrimination here, as that would be illegal. But if you buy three bedroom, two bath homes *only,* it's much less likely that any single people or roommates will be answering your ad for renters, as they tend to prefer apartments anyway. And singles and roommates are much more likely to want just one or two bedrooms. And if they come to your neighborhood and see kids having fun playing kickball on the street, the singles and roommates generally aren't going to be dying to live in a neighborhood of children anyway, because they just aren't at that stage of their lives yet. So buying the three bedroom homes virtually eliminates the singles and roommates for rental applicants, and generally most of your rental candidates will be families.

Also, by buying what is basically considered an entry-level "starter" home, everyone and his brother will be among your potential buyers should you ever need to sell. And the house will be easier to qualify for a loan than that $750,000 six-bedroom mini-mansion down the block! Plus, the smaller the house, the lower the taxes, the lower the insurance costs, the lower your tenants' utility bills, and the lower the repair and repainting costs will be after your tenants move out. And the lower your expenses are, the more rent money can go into your pocket! Furthermore, the rent you can get on a larger house usually isn't much more than what you can get on an entry-level unit, although the expenses are *much* higher on the bigger places. Not to mention that the purchase price for larger units is much higher, too.

Another piece of advice. Never buy a two-bedroom unit, or a "two bedroom with a den" property. In order to qualify as an actual "bedroom" for Section 8 (more about Section 8 later), all bedrooms *must* have a door to close them off from the rest of the house, and all bedrooms *must* have a closet. Most "dens" don't meet that qualification. Also, if the time ever comes that you want to sell your property, the most popular, easiest and fastest homes to sell are always the three bedroom, two bathroom starter homes. If you ever want to sell your properties, and sell them fast, these are what sell, and virtually everyone can afford them.

HOAs – Avoid Them Like the Plague!
Before I had perfected my criteria for the best rental properties to buy, I made a mistake and purchased many condos in various different Home Owner Association communities

(HOAs). In theory, I thought they were a great idea. After all, plenty of curb appeal, no common areas to maintain, the association takes care of keeping the landscape pretty, they paint the condos as needed and repair the roofs, they maintain the roads in the complex, and you can offer your tenants the special amenities of access to a pool, spa, a workout facility and often a gated community. It all seems like a lot of extra value to your tenants, which should translate to higher rents, less maintenance costs to you, and happy, long-term tenants. It *seems* like that would be the case. But it's not!

I soon found out that the residents of *most* HOA communities have a *huge and very nasty* bias against renters. The residents of most of the associations I dealt with harassed my tenants mercilessly, bombarding both me and my tenants with "alleged" violation letters on an almost daily basis. While maybe 1% of the violation letters were legitimate complaints, most were just bogus in a blatant attempt to get my tenants to leave and to get me to sell my properties. That led to a high turnover rate with my good-paying, responsible tenants. No tenant wants to stay in a hostile environment!

That led to less profitability for me, not to mention the aggravation of constantly having to correspond with or appear before the HOA Board of Directors to defend my actions and those of my renters. HOA communities do have plenty of curb appeal, but there is definitely no welcome wagon – more like a firing squad to greet your new tenants! So I cannot urge you strongly enough – *no HOA units!*

Don't Deviate From a Winning System!

Finding the right property that meet your criteria as listed above is the most important step for success as a landlord. The second most important step? Running the numbers. If the numbers don't add up, it's not the right rental for you. Don't get caught up in the "But it's so pretty!" trap. Pretty might win a beauty contest, but it's not going to assure your success as a landlord. If the unit doesn't fit your criteria, you'll regret making a bad financial decision based upon an emotional response.

Remember my motto: Good is good enough for tenants. And my criteria is *plenty* good enough for my tenants – why else would so many of them stay with me for years and sometimes decades? You aren't trying to find a palace or high class mansion to use as a rental. Run the numbers first. I'll show you examples later in this chapter to show you how. If the numbers don't work, don't buy. The last thing you want to do on your road to financial freedom is tie yourself to a rental property that's a loser. Especially when there are so many properties out there that are winners that can provide a great positive cash flow!

Where to Begin Your Search

Newspaper ads? Realtors? "For Sale" signs in the window? Where's the best place to begin your search for a rental house? I've used a couple of different methods over the years, but in the end I prefer working with a real estate agent. The one "for sale by owner" property I bought actually went pretty smoothly because the seller was a real estate agent. If she hadn't been an agent, it could have easily ended up going sideways.

Besides, as the buyer, *you're* not paying the commission, the seller is. So why not take advantage of the agent's free expertise and guidance, not to mention the opportunity to obtain a free rental application and lease from your agent? (More on the application and lease later.) After all, it's the least he can do for you after you've just made him a 3% commission by buying a house from him!

Of course, all of this brings up the question of how to find a good agent. There are plenty of really lousy agents out there. But once you buy your first house (even if it's the one you live in yourself), you'll have a pretty good idea of how the whole process works, as well as what's important to look for in the contracts. Most real estate contracts are boilerplate - that is, standard from one contract to the next. But you want to make sure that the *purchase price* is what you agreed to pay, the *down payment, amount financed and the fixed interest rate on your mortgage* are all what you agreed to pay, and that the *closing costs* are what you agreed to pay, and that any extras like a *home warranty* is included if you agreed to it, and that it's being paid for by whichever party agreed to pay for it. Also make sure that the *close of escrow date* is what you agreed to, and that you have 10 days for *due diligence.* Due diligence is when you conduct any inspections you need and re-run the numbers, to make sure you still want to proceed with your deal. Generally, you can get out of the contract for virtually *any* reason during the "due diligence" period.

Finding a good agent is not easy. To do that, I'd start by asking friends and family members for referrals. If you know someone in the business of real estate rentals, ask him who he uses. It's likely he will have done a lot of repeat business and has settled on a really great agent.

The first few agents I dealt with were mediocre at best, but my current agent is the best I've ever had. I found him through a newspaper article. He was new in town and new to real estate. He was also in the process of investing personally in rental properties in Las Vegas. I called him, took him to lunch, and interviewed him. Despite his lack of years in the business, he was the most knowledgeable agent I've ever met. I send him a ton of referral business.

Just as with any professional you use, I suggest you interview several of the agents your friends or associates recommend and tell them what you're trying to accomplish. Then sit back and see what they have to say. Often real estate agents have good connections with mortgage brokers, so ask about that, too. An agent who can help smooth the way with loan processing is a huge help!

After interviewing a few agents, you'll have a good feel for who knows his stuff and who doesn't. You'll also get a feel for which agent actually *cares* about helping you reach your investment goals, as opposed to someone who wants to sell you the first house you see just to make a quick commission.

You don't have to take the agents you interview to lunch, of course. You can simply schedule an interview at their office. Wherever you meet, make sure it's quiet enough to do some serious talking without interruption.

My number one piece of advice when choosing an agent? Don't go with anyone who tries to "hard sell" you. *Ever.* My next piece of advice - never *ever* choose an agent who's working for you *and* the seller. If your agent asks you if you mind if he represents both of you in a deal, *run for the hills!* He can't possibly protect *your* best interests if he has already promised to protect the *seller's* best interests. See what I mean?

You want what is called a "buyer's agent." Yes, he can still list all the properties he wants from other clients, but he won't be selling you a house he listed himself, because the only person he's representing in that deal is himself, since he stands to collect a double commission. Realtors even have a legally required form (a waiver) saying that it's "okay" for them to represent both parties (buyer and seller) in the deal. The reason for the legally required waiver is because even the *state laws* recognize that a realtor working for both you and the seller is a *huge conflict of legal interests.* If you sign that waiver, you are signing away your legal rights to be fully represented by your real estate agent. Absolutely refuse. If your agent wants to sell you a house, he has to work *only* for you, protecting only *your* best interests.

Discuss his feelings on this issue at your initial interview. Trust is something you need to develop after interviewing several agents. The interviews should produce a couple of losers and a couple of winners. Just as in choosing an attorney, a business broker, or a CPA, as you interview the realtors, you'll soon begin to get a feel for who knows his business best. You'll also realize who is more interested in helping you achieve your goal of retiring as a landlord, and who simply wants to hard sell you to crank out a fast, easy commission.

If your potential agent leaves you feeling as if you just dealt with a used car salesman, go home, shower off the sleaze, and move on to the next interviewee on your agents' list. But if your potential agent leaves you with a warm fuzzy feeling, as though he really cares about helping you reach your goals, *and* he really knows his stuff, that's the guy you want.

What an Agent Will Do

Once you settle on an agent, you should have a realistic expectation of what he can and can't do for you. Here are a few things I've learned over the years.

First, if you've found a good agent, he's going to want to do whatever you ask of him. It's human nature. But the bottom line is that he only has so much free time to devote to you, so don't abuse his good nature. Remember, you'll be looking at a ton of different properties, especially early in your search. They'll all be relatively inexpensive homes, much more so than the norm, which means the agent's commission will be small in comparison to other sales he makes. Of course, in the long run, he'll make more off you in commissions on 10 to 20 rental houses than he would on a single $500,000 home sale to Joe Show Off. But those commissions from you will take considerably more time and paperwork, because they'll involve 10 – 20 little deals instead of one big one. So be considerate of his time. All good business relationships show respect both ways. Give him your criteria for rental houses, and he can program that into his computer. Whenever a unit fitting that criteria comes on the market, his computer will automatically email you the info.

Again, be considerate of your agent's time. *You* need to look at the listing paperwork your agent sent you on your computer and run the numbers before you ask to see a house. In that way, if the numbers don't work, you won't be wasting the agent's time (and yours) by asking to see it. When you find a house for which the numbers *do* work out, run a "drive by" on your own, without your agent. Drive slowly around the neighborhood. See if most of the houses in the area have curb appeal. If you were a renter driving through the neighborhood, would *you* want to rent in that area, or would you be focused on those dead cars on cinder blocks in one driveway after the next?

Once you've done a drive-by and found the neighborhood to be desirable, call your agent to schedule an appointment. He should bring all the forms for your purchase agreement with him. If you decide to proceed, you can sign right then and there and get things going, saving you both time. Or if you need more time to think about it, you can take the forms home with you while you consider your decision.

He should also bring comps (recent comparable property sales prices) for all the other houses in the neighborhood so you can see what the most recent house sales have brought. Usually comps are in the form of dollars per square foot. Depending on your specific market - some areas are still trending downward on prices, while other areas of the country are starting to go back up or have remained the same - I'd ask your agent for his recommendation on the asking price, and why he came to his conclusion on the price.

If you're paying cash, you can often come in under list price if prices are still trending downward. If prices are trending upward, you may want to offer list price. If you're financing the purchase, you are generally less attractive to the sellers - most of which are banks these days. So, your offer may need to be a little higher than asking price to be given serious consideration. This is something your agent should be able to guide you on, as he should have his finger on the "hot button" of your particular area's real estate climate.

Another word of advice - I'd tend to shy away from an agent who is reluctant to give you a price recommendation. You don't have to follow his recommendation, of course, but he should have an opinion and be willing to share it with you, along with his rationale for his recommendation. This is your real estate agent's business after all, and he is being paid for his expertise. If he is unwilling to share that expertise, then *why* is he your agent?

If you find yourself unsure about the house for any reason whatsoever, take the purchase agreement with you to mull over. Don't ever feel pressured to sign *anything*. Go home and think about it. Sometimes, a house can fit your criteria perfectly, the numbers work out great, the neighborhood is attractive, but for some reason, you just have a bad gut feeling. I have learned to always trust my gut feelings. Whenever I don't, bad things happen. There will be plenty of homes that suit your criteria, so if you simply don't like one for whatever the reason, just say no!

Running the Numbers

Once your agent finds you a rental property, how exactly do you "run the numbers" to decide if it's going to provide a good return on investment?

The first thing I do when I print out a new listing sheet from my agent is to check the asking price, the annual taxes, a home owner's insurance policy estimate, which you can get from your insurance agent, and the sewer and trash expenses, which are likely to be the same for all homes everywhere in town, regardless of the size or location of the house.

Whenever you run the numbers, always assume the worst case scenario. If that worst case scenario were to come true and you find that the house is still a good deal, you'll be fine. But if worst case scenario is really bad or scary, or even just "on the edge," just say no and walk away. Usually life hands you something between worst case and best case, and the more prepared you are for the worst, the closer to best case scenario is likely to happen.

As an example, let's say you're considering a house listed at $94,000. You haven't seen the inside of the house yet, but assume the worst. Let's pretend it's going to need $3,000 worth of cosmetic work to make it rent ready - although likely it will need less. Add to that figure another $3,000 for closing costs. This amount will vary from state to state, depending upon what is standard in your state for the buyer to pay for at close of escrow vs. what the seller pays for. You can ask your real estate agent what you can expect your closing costs to be for the houses you're shopping for in your price range. Now your total cost to get into the house is $100,000. Here are the numbers:

$100,000 - Total costs to buy the house and prepare for tenants.
$30,000 - Your 30% down payment with a mortgage for the balance.

$1,200/month – The amount your research shows you can expect for rent. (More on how to determine rents in your area later).

$403/month - Mortgage payment for a $70,000 loan at 5.62% interest.

$50/month - Property tax.

$23/month - Sewer and trash costs.

$50/month - Homeowner's insurance cost

$50/month - Repairs and maintenance – This is money you will save each month but may not need for quite some time. It's a good hedge against expenses. And it's good to save this money every month, in case of a sudden expensive repair, like an air conditioner unit needing repair – you'll be prepared, so no big deal!

$624/month - Net profit before depreciation and income taxes on this property.

So is this a good investment or a bad one?

I look at any property that nets $500/month or more on a $30,000 down payment to be a great deal. A net profit of $624 a month translates to $7,488 a year. With the $30,000 down payment you paid toward the purchase of the property, that translates to just shy of 25% return on investment (ROI), which is a *fantastic* return. Compare that to the interest rate that you can get from your bank on a Certificate of Deposit!

Now, let's assume you found a house that fits your rental property criteria, but it costs $150,000. Assume $3,500 in closing costs because a more expensive home will have higher closing costs. Also assume $5,000 for your punch list. "Punch list" is fancy contractor speak for your "repair list," which is very likely more expensive for a more expensive home. So now you're looking at the following numbers:

$158,500 - Total costs to buy house and prep for tenants.

$47,550 - Required for a 30% down payment, which takes longer to save up, so you are wasting more time *and* money to get that first rental property.

$1,200/month – Expected rental income as per your prior research.

$638/month - Mortgage payment for a $110,950 loan at 5.62% interest.

$80/month - Homeowners insurance - a more expensive house costs more to insure.

$85 - Property taxes - generally based on purchase price, therefore a more expensive home has higher property taxes.

$23/month - Sewer and trash costs.

$80/month - Repairs and maintenance - because this home is more expensive, it is likely larger, which means higher repair and maintenance costs.

$294/month - Net profit before depreciation and income taxes on this property.

Is *this* house a good rental-property investment?

It nets $3,528 a year, which is only slightly more than a 7% return on your initial investment of $47,550. That's cutting things awfully close to the edge. This is a deal from which I would *run*, I don't care how pretty the house or the neighborhood is. You're not making enough return for it to be worth your while. And while 7% is still a decent return, and certainly better than a bank certificate of deposit is paying these days, why would you choose to make only 7%, when you can make 25% instead? The more you make (and then keep!) the faster you retire!

Bottom line: Stick to my formula. It's easy to follow. It works. It's a proven winner. Remember, it's not broke, so don't fix it!

A Word on Depreciation

Another wonderful aspect of landlording is depreciation. Depreciation is a tax deduction that works in your favor. Each year, after calculating your income and then deducting your expenses, your CPA will also calculate and deduct depreciation from your rental income. The IRS allows for you to deduct approximately 3% a year on the initial cost of your rental property. So if the initial cost of your rental property was $100,000, then your CPA will deduct $3,333 off of your rental income after all expenses. In our initial example of a great house deal, where your net rental income after expenses was $7,488 a year, you won't be paying taxes on that full amount! Oh no! Your CPA will *legally* deduct your depreciation ($7,488 – $3,333 = $4,155). So you'll only actually be paying taxes on $4,155, not on the $7,488 you actually made! So you will be essentially making even more money because you won't owe it in taxes. Along with paying taxes on significantly less than your full rental income, this will also help to place you in a lower tax bracket, saving you even more money on taxes. Remember the old saying, "A penny saved is a penny earned?" Well I believe that "Taxes not paid is money that's made!"

    I have 21 rental units as of the time this book was written, so I get to deduct roughly $73,000 a year off my taxable income each year – which significantly reduces my "taxable income" which saves me a tremendous amount on taxes to start with, and then drops me into a much lower tax bracket as well – which leaves me even *more* money to invest in even more retirement assets! Are you starting to see all the multiple ways that investing in real estate is such a wonderful, safe and highly profitable way to go? Good!

Milage Logs...Again!

    I want to also mention that just like for your service business, you get to keep a "milage log" for your rentals as well. Update your milage log every time you look at a potential piece of real estate for investment, every time you go to a closing or visit your insurance agent, every time you show a unit to a prospective tenant, every time you go collect your rent, every time you inspect a unit, every time you deposit your rents in the bank, every time you drive over to do maintenance or repairs. If you are handy enough to do any maintenance or repairs yourself, that is! Remember, you don't need to be a handyman yourself to be a successful landlord. I'm just a skinny, unskilled girl (as far as repairs and maintenance go) and I'm doing just fine!

Check with your CPA to be sure of all the requirements, but basically your milage log will need to have the following details – the date, the place you went and why, and the milage. And remember to record absolutely *every trip* you make that is involved with your rental properties. The IRS allows for a healthy re-imbursement for each mile you drive, and by keeping this log on a daily basis, you then end up with another healthy *legal* deduction against your profits, which is also deducted from your "taxable income," just like the depreciation expense is. And it may very well drop you into a lower tax bracket as well. Again, less taxes paid equals more money made!

Ready-Made Rental Units

People often ask me if it's a good idea to buy a property that is already in the rental pool, one which already has renters living in it. After all, it seems as though that would provide you with income from the day you sign your closing papers - without having to go through the hassle and expense of cleaning, painting and repairing the property or finding renters yourself.

Sounds reasonable, doesn't it? But the truth is I've only ever bought two tenant occupied rental units in my life, and I won't do it again.

Instead of buying a ready-made source of income, I simply bought someone else's "problem child." Pre-existing tenants often pay rents that are way too low to make owning the house profitable. Many don't pay on time. Some don't pay at all. Think about it. If a landlord had excellent tenants who were paying good money right on time, why on earth would he *ever* sell the house so long as it continued functioning as a no-hassle cash cow?

The tenants I inherited with those purchases aggravate me to no end. I'd get rid of them in a heartbeat if I could – but they also came with a lease I have to honor until it expires or until they violate it sufficiently to evict them. But I learned with those experiences that the best way to get rid of a bad tenant is never to let them into your property to begin with. I have a good system for selecting tenants, and I won't ever deviate from that system again. Here I ignored my gut feelings, strayed from my own business rules, and I paid the price. These were *my* mistakes from which *you* can learn!

Handling Buyer's Remorse

I'm not perfect, and they say the best way to learn is to make mistakes. Well, I've made quite a few in my lifetime, and I've learned a lot. Now I want you to benefit from my mistakes and, hopefully, avoid making them yourself.

What is buyer's remorse? It's that after-the-fact feeling that you shouldn't have bought something after you bought it. If you have a strong gut feeling about backing out during the due diligence period, do so. Listen to your gut. So long as it's during the time period when you have the right to back out with no legal ramifications, you should be able to get your earnest money deposit back. No harm, no foul.

I regretted buying the homes with the tenants already in them, but I failed to listen to my gut. I let the due diligence period pass, and I went through with the deals. Sometimes a house can meet all of your criteria. It can be the right house, the right neighborhood and the right financials, but for some reason it just "feels wrong."

Trust me. Trust your gut.

For me, if a house meets all my business criteria *first and foremost*, then I know it's a good buy. But I know it's a great buy if it meets all my business criteria *and* I also fall just a little bit in love with it. If I feel the urge to live there, if it feels like a home I would want to live in personally, I'm generally *very* happy with my purchase.

It's something I call "There's no place like home" factor. Remember, if you'd live in it, and it meets all of your investment property requirements, it's a good deal. In the worst case scenario, remember that you should be comfortable living in any one of your rental properties, because one day you just might have to.

You can never tell about the future. You can never predict what's to come. If you keep that in mind as you go through life acquiring rental properties, you'll always be comfortable in your own skin, as well as in your own house. No matter *which* one of them it may happen to be!

CHAPTER FOURTEEN

The Importance of Homeowners Insurance

Ok, now you've found the first rental property you want to buy. It fits all the criteria I provided you in the prior chapter. And you've had a *CLUE* report run by your insurance agent to make sure it's insurable, and to learn about any prior claims that might make you want to walk away from this house during the due diligence period in your real estate purchase agreement contract.

So far everything looks good, and you're ready to move forward. Insurance seems like an easy thing to get – don't you just call the same guy who does your auto insurance? Maybe, maybe not. Here are some things you'll want to consider before making your decision.

Personal Insurance Agent or Commercial Insurance Broker?

Most people buy their auto insurance from a personal

insurance agent, like all the personal agents you see advertising on tv. Whether it's a famous lizard trying to sell you insurance or someone with good hands or someone who is especially neighborly, these agents are just personal insurance agents, not commercial insurance brokers. So what's the difference?

There are many differences. A personal insurance agent deals only with his company's insurance policies and their specific pricing. A personal agent is not able to shop around for you with other insurance companies to get you the best insurance coverage and rates for your particular situation.

A commercial insurance *broker,* on the other hand, has access to *all* the commercial insurance companies. And in general, you can get more coverage and at cheaper rates from a commercial insurance broker than you can from your local personal insurance agent just down the street. Also, your commercial insurance broker can also insure your personal vehicles, your personal home, your major medical, your bonding and your liability insurance, just as we discussed that you will be purchasing in other chapters.

So along with better coverage and better pricing, you will also get one stop shopping. One thing you may or may not get is better service. Only you can decide that based on the relationship you build with the insurance agent or broker that you choose.

I have worked both with a commercial insurance broker for all of my insurance needs and my local personal insurance agent as well. And here is what I have discovered. The commercial insurance broker was able to provide slightly move coverage for me, on all my 21 rentals, my other three properties that are not rentals, and coverage on my jeep, all for about $1,000 a year *less* than my personal insurance agent. Which is a large amount of savings for slightly better coverage!

But I still choose to go with my local insurance agent. And for me, the reason was customer service. I would rather pay more money for better customer service. That way there is no frustration for me. I like everything to be smooth and easy for me. All I have to do with my great personal insurance agent is to call him up and say "I need another "Aimee policy" for this address, effective date to be (whatever my close of escrow date is)."

My agent knows exactly what coverages to set up for me, he sends me a bill and an insurance binder and I am good to go. I know we are on the exact same page, and he doesn't bother me with the same questions over and over for each application, he just handles it on his end. He knows my criteria for rental properties and knows what I'm buying and any information he doesn't have he gets off the county tax assessors website – he isn't bothering me for it.

Also, as I always advise, I read over every policy to make sure I understand what I am buying, what coverages I am getting, and under what circumstances I should file a claim and how the entire process works. Now, insurance companies are written much like legal documents – only "insurance legalese" (as I call it) is *twice* as hard for me to understand than any other type of business contract.

So I always write down my questions, and then I zap my local insurance agent an email asking my questions. He will send me back easy to understand explanations, using simple examples, and that sets my mind at ease. Because now I not only know what I'm buying, but I also know I'm buying the appropriate coverages for me.

However, when I tried to do the same thing with my commercial insurance broker, when there were questions about what the insurance documents meant she treated me completely differently. I would do the same with her and send her an email to ask what certain language meant. Instead of giving me an easy to understand explanation, she would refer back to the paragraph I couldn't understand and tell me to "read it."

I explained that I had already done that and couldn't understand what it meant. And still she refused to give me any explanation other than "read that paragraph again."

I have a firm belief that if any sales person, whether an insurance agent or financial advisor or real estate agent, either *cannot* or *will not* explain the item I am purchasing in five minutes or less in a way that makes sense to me, using words that any ten year old can understand, then something is fishy.

It's possible they don't understand what they are selling. Which tells me that they don't even know if what they are selling me is appropriate. Or they could just be trying to sell me whatever generates the highest commission for them. Or they are just uneducated, uninformed and shouldn't be in the business of selling that product to anyone. Or they are just lousy at customer service.

Whatever the reason, I find it highly offensive that an insurance broker would flat out refuse to give me a simple example to explain a paragraph to me. I understand that the insurance documents will govern in the case of a claim. But if this is a sales person with many years of expertise who refuses to share that expertise, I find that position to be unreasonable and irritating to the point that I will take my business elsewhere.

After all, I'm *not* just paying for the insurance, I'm also paying for their expertise, their customer service and the happy business relationship that I want to have when dealing with that person. I am not looking to argue with or be stonewalled by my vendors.

As a new business owner, and new rental property owner, certainly I would recommend to you to buy the cheapest policies you can get. Your budget is your top priority when you are first starting out, and you need to watch the pennies very closely. And in reality, the coverage from the commercial broker is likely to be almost identical to the coverage you get from the personal broker. It's just cheaper, which is a very good thing!

But now that I've "made it," I make sure that I deal with people who make me happy to work with them. At this point in my life, I prefer to work with the agent who gives me the better service. And for the extra $1,000 a year for 24 properties and my jeep coverage, that works out to just about $4 a month extra per policy. I consider that a small price to pay to enjoy my business relationship.

Since I no longer have to worry about money, I can pay a little extra for the privilege of better customer service and a happy business relationship. I like dealing with someone who feels more like a friend instead of dealing with someone who makes me feel like a nun is about to hit my knuckles with a ruler for even daring to ask a question.

See, it works both ways – make a friend, make a sale. My personal insurance agent understands that, and because of his friendly and happy-to- be-helpful attitude, he gets my commissions instead of the commercial agent. Smart man!

Insurance Deductibles – How High Can You Go?
Another aspect to consider on your rental property coverage, is to get the highest deductible you can comfortably afford and that your mortgage lender will allow. Since you are financing your properties, your mortgage lender will dictate exactly what the highest deductible you can have will be. But with a 30% down payment, it shouldn't be hard to get a nice high deductible. Doing so will dramatically reduce your insurance premiums.

Part of the "Aimee Package" that my personal agent knows is standard for me, is that I get a $10,000 deductible on all of my rental properties. This is because I know I can pay for minor incidents. And if you use your homeowners insurance policy as a "maintenance" policy, you will quickly find that your policies are either cancelled, non-renewed or your rates will increase greatly – none of which is desirable. And good luck finding new, cheap homeowners insurance on a property that has already had several claims on it by you as the owner.

Remember those *CLUE* reports I mentioned? Well, the insurance companies share them with each other as well. They will check if you have had past claims on your properties, and there is no hiding it if you have filed claims in the past. Besides, since you are going to keep a $10,000 reserve fund on your properties (we'll discuss this later), you'll easily be able to cover most small incidents yourself.

Just like your catastrophic / major medical insurance policy, you want to keep a large deductible to keep your rates low. And try to only file claims on your homeowners insurance in the case of something catastrophic – like a fire, where part of your rental needs to be rebuilt and to remediate the smoke damage from the non-burned portion of your home.

In my approximately twelve plus years of landlording, I have only filed one insurance claim on one rental. And that was against my better judgment. I had foolishly decided to go the more impersonal route of a commercial broker, and I had some water damage at one of my units. I had never had this happen before, and so didn't know if I should file a claim or not. And if the answer was yes, I didn't know if I needed to get the insurance company's ok before sending out my guys out to do the repairs. But being water, I also didn't want to wait to dry the place out while the insurance company hemmed and hawed, as I didn't want any mold to grow.

So my commercial broker insisted I should file a claim. I was reluctant, but I followed her advice, since I had no idea of how much the water damage would cost to repair. And I also couldn't get a straight answer out of the insurance lady as to whether or not I was required to use their recommended vendors for the repair or if I could use my own. As it turned out, the damage was only around $3,100, and it was perfectly fine to use my own personnel. My deductible on this property was $2,500 (for whatever reason, this policy wouldn't offer a $10,000 deductible). Long story short, the insurance company ended up paying me only $600 on my claim. But now my insurance rates for that property have doubled.

And how long do you think it will take the insurance company to re-coup their $600? Just a couple of years, but I'll be paying that extra money each year for the insurance until the end of time – or until I sell the unit. *And* that property now has a documented record of water damage, to be shared with every insurance agent on the planet, which makes selling and future insurance even more expensive.

Had I been dealing with my neighborly great local personal insurance agent, he would have advised me to go ahead with the repair, and if the bills were too high for me, to *then* file a claim, which I never would have done for as little as a $3,100 repair. Lesson learned for me! Another time when I ignored my gut instincts and paid the price – which means it's time again for you to benefit by learning from my mistake!

Umbrella Liability Insurance

As you become more and more successful, you will need to consider umbrella liability insurance. Just as your service business is covered by a commercial liability policy, to protect you from any claims of injuries to your customers, you will need an umbrella liability policy to protect you from any renters who want to sue you for any injuries (real or imagined) while living in your home. The recommended rule of thumb is to purchase an umbrella policy in an amount equal to your net worth at that time. So calculate your total net worth.

This will include the equity in your personal residence and in all of your rental properties, the value of your service business, the value of any bank accounts that you have and any other assets you have accumulated by now. Let's say your net worth is $700,000 by now. Then you will want to buy an umbrella liability policy for that same amount.

That way if someone wants to sue you for all you are worth, your insurance will protect you from that happening. And believe me, the insurance company has fantastic, determined, aggressive lawyers fighting on your behalf, so that the insurance company pays out as little as possible. But just as with your catastrophic health insurance, you always want to have enough coverage to protect the fabulous retirement nest egg you are building. You don't want one greedy tenant trying to retire off of all *your* hard work due to a frivolous lawsuit. Be smart and protect yourself.

Lawsuits and How to Avoid Them

Ok, now that I have scared you into getting that umbrella liability policy, let me share with you the following. In all of my eighteen years of service business ownership, *not once* did anyone ever sue me for anything. In all of my twelve plus years of landlording, *not once* has anyone ever sued me for anything.

I am a firm believer that this is the case for two reasons. One is that I always go above and beyond the call of duty. So none of my customers or tenants were ever harboring secret resentments towards me for not doing my job properly. It's when people feel abused or disrespected that they want to retaliate with a lawsuit. Which is why I always advocate doing the very best job possible and treating the customer like gold, even when they are in the wrong.

The second reason I believe I have never been sued (along with there being no legitimate reason to do so) is because of "Make a friend, Make a sale." My tenants and prior business clients saw me as a friend, and friends are people you are loyal to. People don't sue friends. People sue cold-hearted businesses that they believe have abused them in some way.

So purchase your umbrella liability policy, and sleep soundly at night. They are extremely inexpensive for all the coverage you get with them. And just like bonding and liability insurance for your service business, they all protect *you*. You don't need one insane client or tenant with a frivolous lawsuit to make your life a financial wasteland. Especially not when you are doing such a fantastic job on your road to financial freedom and early retirement!

CHAPTER FIFTEEN

Funding Your First Rental Property

    I had been thinking about getting into real estate investing ever since my first foray into landlording with that two bedroom apartment I had with all the roommates - imagine making money as a landlord on a property you don't even own! I thought that was the neatest "job" ever.
    But I have also always been very risk averse. I only like to earn my money once, and I get very upset with myself when I've made the occasional bad financial decision that caused me to lose even a little of my hard earned cash. But I have always learned from my mistakes. And part of my goal in writing this book is so that *you* will benefit from my learning experiences. I want you to have smooth sailing and great success from day one!
    As a result, once I find a business formula that works, I stick with it. So before I got back into being a landlord, I wanted to find a system that would work for *me*. So I did a lot

of research on every aspect of the rental business, which includes how to find the best funding, and how to protect yourself at close of escrow.

Finding a Trustworthy Mortgage Broker

First you'll need to find a good mortgage broker. You will do this the same way you found your CPA, attorney and real estate agent. Ask for referrals from friends and family, from people who are already landlords, and also from your real estate agent. Interview several, telling them what you want to accomplish, and ask if they have investor loans that can suit your needs. Then sit back and listen to what they have to say. Take notes to compare with the other mortgage brokers you interview. Who seems to know his business the best? Who has the best loans available for you at the best interest rates? Ask what they would recommend for you. Their answers will tell you if this is the right mortgage broker for you. As always, you want to choose someone with great expertise in their field, who has *your* best interests at heart, and that you will enjoy working with.

Here are some critically important things to know about loans and funding, that will help you decide if this mortgage broker is out to help you or only help himself instead...

Choosing the Right Loans

When it comes to funding your purchase, never accept a loan that includes a "pre-payment penalty." If fortune smiles upon you and you want to pay off your loan early (and save buckets of money in monthly interest costs), then why should you be penalized for doing so? If your service business sells for more than you ever dreamed, you would be wise to pay off any mortgages you have, without penalty. And by the way, those pre-payment penalties often run into the several thousand dollar range. I would stay away from any mortgage broker who wants to sell you a mortgage with a pre-payment penalty included.

Another point about loans – at close of escrow, always check to see that the interest rate is what you agreed upon.

Rates sometimes have a mysterious way of increasing from what you discussed verbally in an informal meeting to what ends up on a mortgage loan contract. Make sure you get it in writing from your mortgage broker that your rate is "locked-in" and won't be changing for at least 30 – 45 days. That's the time it usually takes for a deal to close from the time the seller accepts your purchase agreement until the time you are in the escrow office, executing all of the documents to make the property yours. Both the principal and interest payments should be what you were told they would be. Likewise, the term (or length of the loan), whether for 10, 15, 20 or 30 years, should be what you agreed upon as well. If you can't trust your mortgage broker to stick to his word, why would you ever want to deal with him? Find a new broker if this ever happens to you.

And always, always, *always* go with a fixed-rate loan *only*. *Never* accept an "interest only loan," which you can pay on for 30 years, after which time you *still* don't own the house, because you still owe the original purchase price! If a broker recommends this type of loan for you, I would run for the hills.

Also, never *ever* do a loan with "negative amortization" or you'll be making super low payments only to end up owing more at the end of the loan than you agreed to pay for the purchase price of the house.

Likewise, *never* do a loan with a "balloon payment" at the end because, in all likelihood, you won't have the money available when it's due. And then you could either lose the home or have to refinance - *if* you can find a new mortgage loan at that time.

If you choose an interest only loan, a negative amortization loan, or a balloon payment loan – you won't own the home after you have made payments for 30 years. And after making payments on a house for 30 years, don't you think you should own the home free and clear? I think you should!

Similarly, never do *any* type of variable-interest rate or ARM loan (ARM stands for Adjustable Rate Mortgage). In this type of loan you receive a low teaser rate (like bait-and-switch). Since interest rates are currently at some of the lowest that they have ever been in history, what direction do you think they'll end up going?

You got it. Up, up and up! That means your monthly mortgage payment will skyrocket, and your profits will disappear. Possibly even throwing you into a negative cash flow situation, which is totally unacceptable.

So do *only* fixed-rate loans, and negotiate the best interest rate possible. You'll be glad you did so later.

By the way, don't get hung up on believing that a 30 year loan is the only option available to you. That's the standard, so most people don't even consider other options. I would never take out a loan for any *longer* than 30 years. But a 15 year loan is also an option to consider when running your numbers. And here is why: A 15 year loan is generally offered to you at a cheaper interest rate, usually at least .50% cheaper than a 30 year loan, because you aren't keeping the money as long – you are paying it back twice as fast. Some people might think that means your payment is twice as high, but that's simply not true. That's because the bulk of mortgage payments are made up of interest, and if you cut off 15 years of interest, that's a huge savings to you. Here is a look at a 15 year mortgage for our sample house that costs $100,000:

$100,000 (cost of house including closing costs & repairs needed)
$30,000 (down payment)
$1,200 (monthly rent)
$558 (monthly mortgage payment on a 15 year loan, 5.12% *fixed* interest rate)
$23 (sewer and trash each month)
$50 (monthly homeowner insurance cost)
$50 (monthly property tax cost)
$50 (monthly repair fund money set aside for future repairs, if needed)

Net Profit: $469/month, before taxes and depreciation.

So is this house a winner or a loser?

$469 a month is just shy of the $500 mark I gave you, and in a 15 year loan situation, I would say it's wise to make an exception to the $500 a month rule. That $469 times 12 months = $5,628 a year, divided by your $30,000 down payment, equals a return on investment (ROI) of 18.76%. While that's not the 25% return on the 30 year fixed rate example, 18.76% is still a great return. And you will have the house paid off in 15 years instead of 30. So after the 15 years is up and your house is paid for, rents will certainly have increased by then, let's say up to at least $1,500 a month. Now your net profit (before taxes and depreciation) is $1,327 a month. That's $15,924 a year. Now, starting in years 16 - 30, you are making a return on investment of 53.08% - and that's more than twice the return than on the house with the 30 year loan!

So it's definitely worthwhile to consider a 15 year loan. Compare the rates, run the numbers, and see how your comfort level is. Both are good, proven ways to get your financial freedom and early retirement. Both carry different risk factors. The 15 year loan gives you $155 less profit each month for the first 15 years. Which is $155 less "cushion" to work with. But, since you are going play this smart and always have a big $10,000 reserve fund for each rental, which you continue to "replenish" at a rate of $50 a month, I personally don't see that as a big risk.

Or you can go the 30 year loan route and make an extra payment to principal each month to turn it into a 15 year loan. Ask your mortgage broker to give you the exact figures for how much extra principal you would need to pay each month in order to pay off a 30 year loan in 15 years. He will have a special "mortgage calculator" to calculate your particular, specific situation. Then if you have a slow month or two, you aren't *obligated* to make that additional principal payment. Either way is a good, safe way to reach your goal. Do what makes you the most comfortable, so trust your gut here. I don't want you having sleepless nights on your road to financial freedom and early retirement. I just want to show you the variety of ways you can get there. And of all the ways I am showing you, there is no *wrong* way to get there.

So now you know how to find a good mortgage broker. You know all the bad loans to stay away from, and you know the good loans that you want to find. When I found my mortgage broker many years ago, once I developed a track record with him, and he saw my abilities (*I Will* and *I Can*), he pre-approved me for anything I wanted. And then he found the loans for me to make it all happen.

No Money Down is a Thing of the Past

It's unlikely that you will be able to find any no-money-down deals again, due to the real estate market crash and all the foreclosures and short sales. Banks have tightened their lending standards, and now they want you have some skin in the game – your own skin! Which is just another word for your own down payment. They want you to have some money in the deal. Banks figure you are more likely to pay your mortgage if you have something to lose – and they are right!

Fannie Mae Deals

However, Fannie Mae still offers something *nearly* as attractive as a no-money-down mortgage. It's a loan program in which you can purchase a Fannie Mae property through one of the agency's approved lenders for only 10% - 15% down. The availability is limited to properties that have been on the owner-occupant market for at least 30 days. After that they become available for investors to purchase. And investors can buy no more than four properties on this loan program. After that, the requirement jumps to 25% - 30% for investor properties – no matter who you buy them from.

As always, I want to "show you the money" – so here is the breakdown of our standard sample house if you are fortunate enough to snag a Fannie Mae investor deal...

$100,000 (cost of house, including closing costs and repairs)

$15,000 (down payment)

$1,200 (monthly rent)

$489 (monthly payment on an $85,000 mortgage, 30 year fixed rate loan at 5.62% interest rate)
$23 (sewer and trash monthly)
$50 (homeowner insurance costs, monthly)
$50 (property tax, monthly)
$50 (saved for repairs, monthly)

Net Profit: $538/month, before taxes and depreciation.

Is this house a good buy?

This is an excellent return financially! You are making over $500 a month in profits. $538 times 12 months equals $6,456, divided by your $15,000 down payment equals an annual ROI (return on investment) of 43.04% - so this is an awesome deal!!!

Contract for Success and Protect Yourself at Close of Escrow!
Once you've found a rental house, you have your funding all lined up, and have agreed to the terms of the purchase with the seller, take the time to read your contracts from start to finish. I recommend *always* reading your contracts, but especially on the very first time you sign either a real estate purchase agreement, a mortgage loan contract and your escrow documents. Read every paragraph, and ask questions on anything you don't understand.

There is a presumption in law – if you sign a contract, it is presumed by the judge that you both *read it* and *agreed to it*. And in reality, why would the presumption be anything less? Who signs contracts without reading them? Who should?

The first time I bought a house, I was in my late 20s, and it was for me to live in. I was terrified of the whole process. There were some 30 pages of fine print documents filled with legalese, so I told my real estate agent and escrow agent at the closing that I would need to read every page. They were both pretty snotty about that, saying that the contracts were "all boilerplate" and vouching for the fairness of everything in it.

I said calmly but firmly, "Maybe it seems that way to you, because this is what you do for a living. But I've never seen any of these contracts before, and I'm going to read *everything* in them before I sign. And I'll be asking you both questions as I go along to make sure I understand it all."

They patronized me, and said that was fine, and then they promptly began talking over my head as I tried to read. So I stopped them and said, "Look, I can't read and understand all of the legalese if you're going to be talking over my head. So either be quiet, or go outside and chat while I read. I'll come get you if I have any questions."

Wow! That did the trick. And did I ever shock the heck out of them! But I was telling them the truth, and they needed to respect my wishes. And they were both being paid quite well to supervise my close of escrow, so they certainly *owed* me their time and attention. I was *their customer,* after all! I've never regretted doing so, either. Because even though it *did* turn out to be all boilerplate, I was protecting myself. And I was also learning for future purchases what these contracts meant. Never take anyone's word for anything – check it all out yourself. I was in that office more than an hour reading, while my real estate agent and escrow officer sat silently by. But so what?

Today, after being a real estate investor for over a decade, I actually *do* know what is boilerplate. So, I often just check out a few specific key areas of the contracts and then sign, and I'm usually in and out in just five minutes. My realtor's contracts are always the same, so there's no need for me to review anything but a few important areas. But I always advise reading all of your entire contracts (mortgage, real estate and escrow documents) before signing, and ask questions until you're satisfied with the answers.

And if you find that something material has changed in the contract that you never agreed to previously, don't sign. Simple as that, just put the pen down and walk away until the mistake is corrected. If everyone who tried to be a "house flipper" or a "pretend landlord" had ever actually read their contracts or loan documents, or ever run the numbers, they would have seen what bad loans they were getting locked into. You have to be responsible and know what you are signing – always!

Back To Your Future Deals...
If you can't find a 10% - 15% deal that fits your needs, you may simply have to hang onto your service business a little longer before selling it for a profit.

But that doesn't mean you'll get stuck working your service business forever before venturing off into Landlording Heaven! You always have the option of training one of your temps to be your manager and have him run your service business. Just be sure to keep a close eye on him at first, to make sure he can not only successfully *maintain* it, but also continue to *grow* your business for you as well!

Once you trust your manager and your business is successfully on autopilot, you can relax for a little while. After you've re-charged your batteries, all the while saving up more money, it's time to start flexing your newly developing landlording muscles. Once your rental units are set up and running, the toughest thing you'll have to decide is what time to take your afternoon nap!

Just make sure you're still in control of the financial end of your service business, and be sure your manager is capable of doing everything else, *including* growing your business. The money that comes in from your service business will continue to pay your monthly bills, and your profits will continue to grow, so long as your well-trained manager follows in your footsteps. And the profits from your rental units will be additional income you can save. And as those profits grow, from both your service business and the rental units, you will generate even more money to apply toward down payments on even *more* rental units.

Once you've bought enough rental units so that the profits from all of them are enough to cover all your monthly bills, you might want to consider visiting a business broker, to see what he values your business to be for when you decide to list it for sale. It will likely take a year or longer to sell. During that time, your service business will continue earning you even more money so you can buy even more rental units.

And when your business finally sells, the proceeds from the sale will provide you with more cash for buying more rentals. So, you should easily reach your goal of early retirement. All with an income that is twice your living expenses, and just continues to go up, up, *up!*

Want to see the numbers? As an example, let's assume the following:

Your service business generates an income of $10,000 a month (twice your personal expenses, which we'll assume for this example to be $5,000 a month). You have already saved six months of emergency funds ($30,000), or you wouldn't have quit your old job!

Now, in eight months, you save $40,000 more from your service business (eight months times the $5,000 a month left over after paying your personal expenses) and buy a rental house for $100,000. You put down 30% in cash ($30,000), keeping $10,000 as a reserve fund for emergency repairs for that house. Most "pretend landlords" flounder on the emergency reserve fund. Here are a couple of examples of why this fund is so important to your success:

The Importance of Reserve Funds

The first example of a rare but expensive emergency would be needing to replace a heating and air conditioning unit that breaks unexpectedly and is unable to be repaired. Tenants absolutely must have access to heat (and a/c if they live in the desert) as a health and safety issue. With your $10,000 reserve fund, that unexpected and expensive repair is no problem for you and you keep a happy tenant. And the new unit lasts another 15 – 20 years, and likely only costs approximately $3,000. You still have extra in your reserve fund, just in case future issues come up. Win-win.

In another example, your tenant lands a better job out of state, and has given his 30 day notice to move. Now you have a vacant unit for as long as it takes for you to clean, paint, possibly re-carpet, do some minor repairs, advertise for a tenant, and then choose the right tenant. All of which takes time and money, as you have to pay for the cleaning, painting and repairs - unless you have the skill set to do all that yourself. You also have to continue to pay your mortgage while you have no tenant. With your $10,000 reserve fund, you are sitting pretty. Again, in worst case scenario, you likely only spend $2,000–3,000. And you still have extra in your reserve fund, for anything that comes up in the future. So you always have peace of mind. No worries! Again, win-win.

So always make sure to keep that reserve fund for repairs. You want to be a Successful Landlord, not a Pretend Landlord!

Watch Your Snowball of Cash Grow!

Meanwhile, your service business continues to grow and generate savings for you so that you should now be making a profit of $11,000 a month. That means you can save another $40,000 in just seven months, since you're now able to save $6,000 a month. So, you buy a second rental property, once again putting $30,000 down and placing $10,000 into another emergency reserve fund for the new house.

By this time you should be earning $12,000 a month, because you're still growing your service business. Remember, "if you're business isn't growing, it's dying." So this time it only takes six months to duplicate your progress and buy another rental house at the same rates.

By now, your service business is likely be making around $15,000 a month, because the larger it grows the faster it tends to grow, as your reputation and word of mouth continues to spread. Which means you're now able to save another $40,000 for yet *another* rental house within only four months.

When your business is making $16,000 a month, you'll be able to save another $40,000 in only 3-1/2 months; at $17,000 income a month, only 3 months. And remember that, with each house you buy for $30,000 down, you're also saving

$10,000 in an emergency reserve fund - money that's nice to have but might never actually be needed!

Now let's take a look at your average $100,000 rental property. I use that figure because that's the average price for the 1,300 square foot, three-bedroom, two-bath ranch units with attached two-car garage in the Las Vegas area that I like to buy. Your typical unit may cost more or less, depending upon where you live and what area you buy your rental properties in. And your rents will follow prices accordingly.

Let's assume rent is $1,200 a month, which is quite reasonable for that size house. And let's assume that all your rental units are occupied - again, not an unreasonable assumption, especially during a tough real estate sales market. To refresh your memory, here's the financial breakdown again:

$100,000 - Cost of House.
$30,000 - Down Payment.
$1,200/month - Rent.
$403/month - Mortgage payment for a $70,000 loan at 30 year *fixed* rate of 5.62% interest.
$23/month - Sewer and Trash.
$50/month - Property Tax.
$50/month - Home Owner Insurance.
$50/month - Monthly Repairs (this is money you save each month in addition to your repair reserve fund, but you may not need to spend it on repairs anytime soon).

Net Profit: $624/month, before taxes and depreciation.

In this example, while still growing your service business (and perhaps using a manager so that the most difficult task you'll face all day is running to the bank to deposit your money), you will have accomplished the following in only 2-1/2 years after having quit your old full-time job:

1. Amassed a six-month emergency fund of $30,000 for your personal living expenses.

2. Purchased six rental houses that are netting you $3,744 a month (that's pure profit, remember!) - *plus* you'll have $60,000 in reserve funds for those six houses in case of emergencies.

3. Built your service business up to making $17,000 a month and still growing.

At this point, you are a seasoned landlord and know what you're doing. So, if I were you, I'd take my $60,000 in reserve funds and buy two more houses for $30,000 down each. You'll still have your $30,000 from your original six months of living expense emergency funds if you need them, *and* you'll have a business earning you $17,000 a month, plus your 6 rentals are earning you $3,744 a month – so your monthly income from rentals and your service business is now over $20,000 a month. Nice job!

If you continue to keep your monthly living expenses no higher than when you first quit your job (for this example, $5,000 a month), there's no reason to fear investing that $60,000 of reserve funds for the purchase of two more rental houses. So now your eight houses are basically paying nearly *all* of your bills. That's eight rental units netting you $4,992/mo after expenses, only $8 shy of your total monthly living expenses.

All from rental income alone.

What Do You Do Now?
So what's next?
For starters, I would take a good long look at my service business. How much is it earning today, and how much will it earn tomorrow? Find a few qualified business brokers and get some evaluations of how much your business is worth *today*. If that number is not enough to get you the extra rental houses you need to retire early, ask the business brokers how much does your business need to be earning in order to sell for "X" number of dollars. And then continue growing your business

until the day you actually sell it, because again, *if you're not growing, you're dying.* And the larger you keep growing it until it sells, the more it's worth!

But before you buy *any* rental property, consider a few tips from my own experience:

1. Make sure your service business is earning a profit of at least twice the amount of your personal monthly expenditures before venturing into your first rental property. And that you still have your six month emergency fund for your own personal expenses. Of course, if you decided to buy your own ready- made service business as mentioned earlier, then I recommend this same financial status before buying your first rental unit.

But I would also recommend giving yourself at least six months to a year of getting your feet wet with your new service business to make sure you are over the "learning curve" and feel fully confident in your abilities to maintain and grow that service business before jumping into real estate. Learning one new thing at a time is enough. And you want to be fully focused on that new service business you purchased to make sure you have learned all you need to know to feel very comfortable with it's future growth before jumping into landlording. Don't spread yourself too thin.

2. Don't sell your service business until *after* you've tried landlording with *at least* one rental property. If you keep your service business, and you later find out that you don't enjoy owning rental properties (although I doubt that will happen), you'll still have your primary source of income to fall back on, and you can always just sell that one rental property. It's always good to keep all your options open!

3. If you find you love landlording like I do, then continue buying rental properties *while* you continue growing your service business. The two go hand-in-hand. It's like a money snowball rolling downhill – the money rolling in just keeps getting bigger and bigger and it comes in faster and faster!

Once you sell your service business, you'll want to buy enough rental houses so that you're earning double your monthly expenses. Then, if there's any money left over from the business sale - and there very well may be LOTS of it - why not pay off the home you live in, your car, and any other debts, including your credit cards? Then your monthly bills can drop to $2,000 a month or less, allowing you to *save* a whopping $8,000 a month or more – and that's $96,000 a year!

Put that extra money into FDIC insured bank Certificates of Deposit or into investment grade tax-free municipal bonds for a steady, no-hassle income stream, so there's no danger of losing any part of your nest egg. Or keep it in a money market account for liquidity, treat yourself to an occasional really nice vacation or some other special treat, and enjoy. You've earned it.

Just make sure to *always, always, always* save a fair chunk of your leftover money each month. Me personally, I like to save 100% of whatever money is leftover each month after I pay the monthly bills and pay myself my spending money. But pretend that you save up even 50% of the $96,000 in the example above – that's still a savings of almost $500,000 after 10 years. And it still gives you almost $50,000 a year of money to just "play with" for luxuries if you want to.

Everyone has a different personality. I live a very fun, happy lifestyle and never deprive myself of anything I want. It just so happens my tastes are not expensive, so I'm not trying to live on a budget. That's just how I am naturally. You will find your "happy medium" – just make sure you always are saving *something* each month, so that you are always ahead of inflation. Remember, other than matters of the heart, money can solve *almost* any problem – so it's always good to be saving more!

CHAPTER SIXTEEN

Finding and Keeping Reliable Tenants

Let's be honest. Landlording is the easiest way I know of making money without breaking a sweat *legally*. But before you can begin placing tenants in your newly acquired rental property, you're going to have to determine what you can realistically expect to charge them. You don't want to charge too little, or you'll be missing out on a lot of extra cash. You don't want to charge too much, or your property may sit unoccupied for months.

How to Determine Your Rental Rates

There are two ways I like to go about determining what to charge for rent. First, I buy a Sunday paper and look in the classified ads section under "Houses for Rent." You'll find the most listings in the Sunday edition. Check for rental properties in the same part of town where your properties are located. Find every comparable house listed and write the prices down.

Add up the total and divide by the number of houses to get the average rental price. That's what I would charge for my property.

Another way is to ask your real-estate agent for a list of comparables (or "comps") in your area. He should be willing to provide them free of charge. Then check the rental units that are comparable in size to yours.

Where the Renters Are

Once you know how much to charge for your rental unit, you'll need to find some suitable renters. Although there are many ways to do so, I personally favor running a newspaper advertisement. I take out an ad for a month at a time. It's less expensive than weekly. And then I can take my time and find the person I feel is just the right tenant for me.

You can also get your real estate agent to list your property free of charge in the realtor computer website with all the areas listings. In that way, all 10,000 agents in your area (or however many there are) will be searching for suitable tenants for you. Generally, whichever real estate agent finds the tenant will take a either a flat fee or a percentage of the security deposit as their finder's fee. My agent, who is also a broker and has a property management division, as well as several rental properties of his own, does it this way and he has never had a vacant unit for more than a day or two of searching.

You can also run a free internet ad on all of the many lists and classified ads available on the web. But my Sunday newspaper ad also runs in several weekly shoppers, which increases exposure, so I'm happy with that. Choose whichever avenue for advertising you feel is best for you. If you are uncertain, you can try them all, then track the calls, and see which form of advertising gets you the best results. I *don't* recommend putting a "*for rent*" sign in the window of your unit because that will only let thieves know the place is unoccupied. You could wind up with vandals or homeless people breaking in, and that's not good. Similarly, keep the blinds or curtains closed so that passersby can't peek in.

Referral Tenants – Good or Bad?

I never recommend "word of mouth" as a way of finding a tenant, either, because I don't want anyone who's a friend, a friend of a friend, or a relative to know I'm looking for renters. Just as it's important to keep your emotional distance from your employees and business clients, it's wise not to rent to people you know so that they don't end up taking advantage of you. Besides, if you ever had to evict them or enforce the contractual terms of your lease, the relationship would be ruined.

If you pick the right stranger, on the other hand, you can end up in a nice, friendly "business" relationship. You don't need to socialize together, but you can still enjoy working closely with your renters.

However, there *is* one exception to the "word of mouth" rule that I find not only acceptable, but actually *desirable.* And that's when one of my current tenants recommends a new tenant to me. That is *wonderful.* In that case, it's usually a friend or relative of my current tenant. Which means they have visited my current tenant often and are happy with the type of units we are offering. Nothing fancy, nice little starter homes in a great part of town. So that's one hurdle cleared. They have also usually discussed with my current tenant the amount of rents I charge, and that's fine with them too, or they wouldn't have called me. Hurdle number two is cleared.

And best of all, they should know from my current tenant what exactly I expect in a tenant. As in, Aimee is pretty easy going on most things (like pets) and she is *great* on maintenance and repair, but pay your rent on time or else she *will* be collecting late fees, no ifs, ands or buts. Basically, my current tenant has "pre-screened" their referral for me! All I need to do is double check their employment and rental history, and I'm good to go. I know the new tenant will have a good attitude and be happy in our rental program. Also, most of my happy tenants *only* want to refer someone to me who will treat *me* right. They don't want me to hold it against them if their referral doesn't work out. So that is the *only* type of referral I will accept, and I am very happy to do so!

What Type of Tenants Do You Want?

A word about the quality of renters you should be looking for. *Don't* look for someone "classy." I don't care how nicely a tenant maintains a place, or how poorly. Once he moves out, you still have the same basic expenses - new (or newly cleaned) carpeting, new or touched up paint, some minor repairs and a "move-out cleaning." The costs are roughly the same. But a "classy" tenant will be forever persnickety and whining about things while living in your unit. They will never be satisfied and always looking for new things to complain about. And they don't usually stay more than the initial lease period, because they are never satisfied and are always looking for someplace "better." And the higher your turnover with your tenants, the less money going into your pockets.

So, do *you* want to be bothered by a constant barrage of phone calls concerning a bunch of imaginary repairs? Or imaginary issues with the neighbors? I want a nice blue-collar family of renters, people who feel that my house is a big step up from whatever house-in-a-horrible-neighborhood where they were living before. I want the tenants to walk in and say, "Oh, we just *love* this place!!! What do we have to do to get it?"

The last person I want as a renter is the one who comes in saying, "Well, the appliances seem awfully old, and the bedrooms are too small, and the countertop is scratched." That person will be a pain in the fanny forever.

Show me a person who expresses an attitude of gratitude, and I'll show you a great tenant. In fact, along with my preferences for blue-collar workers with families, I prefer a tenant who is at least slightly disorganized and living paycheck to paycheck. He's unlikely to *ever* save enough money to buy a home of his own, and moving is always expensive. Which means if I treat him right, I'll likely have him for a renter for a very long time. Most of my tenants are long term, which is what you should strive to find. The longer a tenant stays, the more profitable he is to you. And the less work. I have tenants who have been with me for a decade. Most have stayed a minimum of two or three years – but that's only because I only started buying back into real estate three years ago – I have every expectation of keeping all the newer tenants for at least a decade as well. *That's* what you want.

Also, check out your prospective tenant's rental application to see how long they stayed at their previous property. I don't want someone who moves every year. I want to find someone who is going to stick around for at least four or five years, somebody who *hates* to move. If you treat your tenants like customers (which they are!), handle their maintenance and repair issues promptly and with a happy attitude, and take care of emergency situations immediately, they'll feel as if you're treating them like gold. And they'll want to stay in your house a long, long time.

No Discrimination

Remember, however, that it is illegal to discriminate against *qualified* tenants. So whatever your "qualifications" are for selecting your tenants, be sure that your qualifications are applied equally and fairly to every applicant. If an applicant meets your standard qualifications, you must accept that tenant. However, bear in mind, that *you and you alone* are the one who gets to decide just *what* your qualifications are. And anyone who doesn't meet those qualifications, you don't have to accept.

But remember, you also *cannot* discriminate against certain protected classes of people. You cannot discriminate against people based on age, race, color, religion, sex, disability, national origin, or familial status. Check with your lawyer to find out the Fair Housing Laws in your state, to find out if any new protected classes have popped up. You don't want to accidentally discriminate without knowing that someone is part of a protected class.

Welfare Tenants

There's yet another place to find tenants for your rental properties. It's called the federal government. One of their programs pays a portion (and sometimes all) of a low-income tenant's rent. The program is called Section 8.

Some landlords fear Section 8 renters. How good can a "welfare recipient" be as a tenant? You might be surprised. Section 8 renters have one major advantage - the United States government guarantees at least part of their monthly payments.

Of course, welfare tenants have their advantages and disadvantages, as do non-welfare tenants who pay the entire rent themselves. It all depends upon the individual renters, which means that, from your point-of-view, it depends upon the strength of their references.

To learn more about Section 8 and what the program might do for you as a landlord, call HUD, the Housing Authority or the Welfare Department in your area. They'll direct you to the local Section 8 office. They'll also give you a "landlord packet" that spells out all the requirements and responsibilities involved in Section 8 renting.

One of the pluses of Section 8 is that if you ever have to evict a tenant due to nonpayment of their portion of the rent, they'll lose their Section 8 benefits *forever*. They'll never be able to enroll in the program again. That's some pretty strong leverage to make sure that they pay their share of the tab on time.

Another plus is that Section 8 screens its program participants to make sure they have no felony convictions - felons aren't allowed to participate. That's a *big* advantage for landlords, since you're not going to want to rent to someone who's running a meth lab in your basement!

The program does require a mandatory inspection of each Section 8 tenant's rental property once a year. The house has to pass, or you'll run the risk of losing your rental payments as well as your tenants. But that annual inspection is a good thing. Sure, you have to be certain your house is up to snuff and meets all government requirements. But you'll also learn how well (or not) the tenant is maintaining your property.

Section 8 notifies you of any "landlord maintenance responsibilities" that you need to correct, and that can be solid preventative maintenance for you. If a Section 8 inspector notices that the hose to your clothes washer is about to burst -

not the tenants' fault, of course - you nonetheless avoid the hassle and cleanup costs simply by replacing a $10 hose before its failure leads to something more costly.

Section 8 Disadvantages

One of the distinct disadvantages of Section 8 is that when the tenants or (more likely) their young children create "tenant damage" - which would be the renters' responsibility to repair - they simply aren't likely to have the money for repairs the way a non-Section 8 tenant might. Let's face it - if your tenants had discretionary funds, they wouldn't be on Section 8!

As a result, you may either have to pay for the repairs yourself, or the tenants will eventually leave sooner than anticipated because the house is now in disrepair, and they don't want to live in the mess they created. Or the home will fail to pass its annual inspection and will be booted out of the program.

And young children are notorious for dropping toys down the toilet, leaving juice stains on the carpet and creating other havoc. If you go the Section 8 route, plan on doing more repairs and paying for them yourself, even if the contract calls for the tenants to pay for them. The question then becomes one of reality. Would you rather pay $50 for a toilet pull, pay $75 to clean the carpet, pay $60 to replace damaged blinds, (even though technically all of these would be the tenants' responsibility) and do whatever else needs to be done? Or would you prefer having your unit vacant for a month or more while you clean up, repair and advertise for new tenants? The choice is yours.

If you choose to do Section 8, don't be penny wise and dollar foolish. Always remember that your tenants are your customers. And *always* remember that it's in your best financial interests to keep your tenants as long as possible. That's what generates the greatest amount of income over the long haul and gives you the least amount of work to do in the end. Treat your customers (your tenants) as if they were gold, and you'll soon be sitting on a pile of gold without a care in the world.

Always remember, your tenants are *not* the enemy. Don't think of them as a bother. Instead let them know you're *always* happy to hear from them and *always* happy to help. Since I have 21 rental units, I keep a full-time handyman on the payroll. Until you own a fair number of homes, you'll probably do best to find a part-time local whom you can trust to do the job. And when your tenants tell you that your handyman said he'd take care of the problem by 7 p.m., make sure that your handyman takes care of the problem by 7 p.m.

Keep Them Happy

All of this comes back to one premise. Keep your tenants happy. Keep them as renters. Why? Because it costs less to maintain an old customer than it does to find a new one. *Always.*

If a tenant wants to give me a 30-day notice, I always ask, "Why? We'd hate to lose you. We *love* having you as a tenant." Then I listen to his response. If it's something I can fix, I *do so.* Perhaps rents have dropped since you first rented to your tenants, or they've had some unexpected bills, or they learn that they can get a similar home down the street for a hundred dollars a month less.

But believe me, they usually don't really *want* to move. People rarely *want* to move. More likely, they feel they *have* to move. It's up to you to remember that it's in your best financial interests (except in the worst possible scenario) to talk them out of it.

So, offer to lower their rent by a hundred dollars a month *if* they'll sign a new two year lease with you. In that way, you'll have the same reliable tenants for another two years, and they'll be happy with the lower rate. It's a win-win situation.

Naturally, there will come a time when there's absolutely nothing you can do to talk your tenants out of moving. Perhaps one of them has a job out-of-state, or perhaps they've finally managed to save enough money to buy a house of their own. Still, *try* to get them to stay. See if there's *anything* you can offer to make them change their minds - or at least postpone the move for a while longer.

I manage to keep my tenants - most of them, at any rate - by handling them with kid gloves. The *very day* they call with a repair or a maintenance issue, I send my handyman out to fix it. So long as he doesn't have to order a part, it's a done deal. If he *does* have to order something, he informs my tenants of how long it will take, and he stays in touch with them, just as I do.

It's called customer service, and it's the name of the game, every bit as important in landlording as it is in running a service business.

Another point to remember. *Never* decide the promptness of service based upon your tenants' payment history. Don't even *think*, "Well, they've paid late the last three months, so I don't have to jump on this." That's what "pretend landlords" do. If you're going to be a *real* landlord, keep your customers happy by going the extra mile. It's not about *you;* it's about *them.*

Most of my tenants tell me, "I don't want to rent from anyone but you," because I treat them so well on maintenance and repair issues, and I always do it with a smile and a warm friendly attitude. Most of my tenants are so grateful afterwards that they actually apologize for having put me out!

Of course, I reassure them that it's my job to take care of them and that I actually *appreciate* them for bringing *any* maintenance or repair issues to my attention, especially while they're still small, so that they don't have a chance to turn into even bigger ones down the road.

What are some of the most common situations landlords face with their tenants? I'll tell you the one you're most often likely to encounter, one that often leads to tenants moving out early.

Pets.

To Pet or Not to Pet

What do you do with tenants who have pets? Or, worse still, what do you do with tenants who say they *don't* have pets, but then pets begin showing up mysteriously days later?

My philosophy has always been that, unless it's a pet that your homeowner insurance policy prohibits (such as a pit bull or an alligator), welcome them. Small dogs, small cats, birds, fish, reptiles. These are things that families with children like, and *families* are what you want for your tenants. Families put down roots, and if renting from you makes them feel like they're living in their own home, they'll want to stay longer, possibly forever.

If you prohibit them from having pets, they'll sneak them in anyway and begrudge you for denying them. And you don't want you tenant to feel like they have to sneak around. You want them to feel that their rental is "their own home."

I understand the issue from the landlord's point-of-view, of course. We all want our property up-kept as well as possible, and not all pets are well-trained. That's one reason I have a clause in my lease regarding pets, and usually tenants who want a pet will ask me how much more it will cost them. If the tenant is someone I like and I'm getting good rent from them, I *don't* enforce the pet portion of the lease. To me, pets are part of the family, and I wouldn't charge my tenants extra if they had another baby. A pet is merely another baby.

On the other hand, if you *want* to get rid of a tenant, enforcing a pet clause is as good a place to start as any.

Clean As a Whistle

Of course, sooner or later, you're going to have tenants move out of your rental unit. That means you're going to have to go in behind them and clean the place up. Possibly repaint. Do some repairs or upgrading, and the best time for that is when the unit is empty. How much do you do, and where do you stop?

My rule of thumb is to do as little as possible. The best motto regarding landlording is "Good is good enough for tenants." If I can simply shampoo the carpet instead of replacing it, I'll do so. I try to get ten years out of a carpet, regardless of the number of tenants. If there's a bad stain, I'll have a carpet repair company swap out a piece from a closet with the stained piece. *Voila!* Carpet that looks as good as new. If there's a bleach stain in the carpet, I'll go to an arts and craft store and buy a magic marker in the color of the carpet to fill in the stain. Unless the carpet is threadbare and worn, I don't replace it. So long as the carpet looks clean and serviceable when you're showing the house, your tenants are likely to be satisfied.

Also, I recommend when it comes time to re-carpet to put in only *dark brown* - as inexpensive as you can find. Dark brown hides all those soft drink and ketchup stains you tenants' kids are bound to create. It also hides oil stains and dirt. All my tenants *love* it, because the carpets always look clean.

With paint, I use a white semi-gloss latex from the local home improvement chain. And I use the same color in all the rooms of all my units. That way, when a tenant moves out, you won't automatically have to paint the entire unit, only those areas that need "touching up." Since all the paint is the same, the new paint should blend nearly perfectly with the old.

My handyman does the painting and any required repairs - and there are always *some* things that need fixing. After that, I have a professional cleaning crew that specializes in "move-out" cleaning for anywhere from $75 - $140, depending on the square footage of the house and the number of bathrooms. Most cleaning can be done quite inexpensively.

On 21 units, I'm doing my first two move-outs in the last three years - not a bad track record. One girl was with me for nine years, has four teenage children, and simply needed a larger place. The same with a second renter. Both were in three-bedroom units, which is a strain on families with four kids. So I understand why they're leaving. We have had such good relationships that they both have tried their very best to leave the units in the same condition as they received them. And I'd be happy to rent to either one of them again.

Finding a Good Rental Contract

Naturally, you can't rent to anyone without a written lease, or rental agreement. Just as you wouldn't enter into a business arrangement with a lawyer, CPA, real estate agent or mortgage broker without understanding the terms and obligations as they relate to both parties, you can't rely upon good will and a handshake when renting.

So, what should the contract contain?

My state's apartment association has a sample lease, and other states probably do as well. But I recommend you check with the real estate agent from whom you purchased your property for a copy of their lease and rental application. All real estate agents have them, and although most leases are boilerplate, some laws differ from state to state. By getting a copy from your agent, you'll have a valid, up-to-date contract free of charge.

As for the variable terms of the lease, I like to make the rent due on the first of the month, because it's simple and impossible to forget. It's also simpler to collect. I offer a grace period for overdue rent that expires at 5 p.m. on the third day of the month. Some landlords don't give any grace period at all. I charge $50 after that, beginning on the fourth day of the month, with an additional $7 a day after that, which keeps accruing until *paid in full*. I may let the pet restriction slide, and I may shoulder more than my fair share of the repair costs, but I let my tenants know that I *have* to have the rent on time or receive adequate compensation.

Of course, I don't really want the late fees, I want to *train* my tenants to pay on time. The late fees merely serve as an incentive to do just that. I always collect every penny due though, *always*. End of story. No negotiation. No excuses. I explain that it's not about wanting extra money, it's about wanting to keep my good credit rating. And if I can't pay my mortgage on time, I have to pay late fees too, and my credit gets whacked.

I'm always pleasant in my explanations, and I make sure I review my late-fee policy with my prospective tenants right up front at the rental interview, before they even fill out the application, so that there's no misunderstanding or confusion later.

How to Collect the Rent

This one seems like a no-brainer, doesn't it? Something you wouldn't think you would need to learn or have lessons on? Actually, successfully collecting the rent is the most important piece of information you need to be a successful landlord. It's also an area where "pretend landlords" flounder the most. Here is what I have learned over the years.

First of all, never let the tenant come to your house to pay the rent. You never want your tenants to know where you live. This is so a disgruntled tenant that you may have had to evict won't come looking for you. Or just so an annoying tenant won't be hunting you down personally if they can't reach you by phone. Also, if you are doing very well in life, you don't want your tenant to see that you live in a mini-mansion and become jealous and resentful of paying their rent. That can quickly spoil the happy business relationship you want to have with your tenants.

Second of all, you never ever want to accept anything but cold hard green *cash* from your tenants. Why? Because cash never bounces. Cash never comes back two weeks later from your bank with "NSF" (Non-Sufficient Funds) stamped on the back of it. Even money orders and cashiers checks are no good. All can be easily forged these days. And if your tenant gives you a cashiers check, they can *still* put a stop payment order on it at the bank to prevent you from getting your money. And again, you won't know until about two weeks later when you get notification from your bank. And you'll also be charged NSF fees from your bank, even though it's not your fault.

It's perfectly legal to demand cash, as it is legal tender. All other forms of checks, money orders and cashiers checks are just IOUs. Those are "promises to pay" but not actual payment. So stick to all cash *only,* no exceptions. Put it in your lease and make it crystal clear to your tenants from day one. And of course let your tenants know that you will always supply them with a written receipt for their payments. That written receipt shows your tenants that you are not trying to pocket their rent money and then illegally evict them.

No one will be offended when you explain that you have had bad experiences with bounced checks in the past, and so your policy is now cash only for everyone. The only people who will be unhappy with your policy are the people who are planning to one day bounce a check with you, and that will help discourage them from even wanting to fill out an application for your rental property. And that's terrific, because you don't want them as tenants anyway!

The next important step is to tell your tenants at the lease signing that if you have not heard from them by the 1st or 2nd of each month, that you will be giving them a little reminder call, as you never ever want to have to enforce the late fee clause on your lease just because they may have forgotten what day it is. And that you are also calling to set up your rent pick up schedule, as you have several homes within five minutes of each other and try to route yourself accordingly to save on gasoline. I am always warm and friendly on my reminder calls, so as not to alienate my tenants.

With this system in place, most of my tenants call me on the first of the month to tell me what day and time is convenient to pick up the rent, which is just terrific! And if they are going to pay late, they let me know so I can mark my calendar. And then I also calculate the late fees for them so they know exactly how much they will need to have ready on the day they are going to pay.

This way you are not sitting home biting your fingernails wondering just *when* or worse yet, *if* will you get your rent. And if anyone hasn't called me by the end of the business day on the first, I am on the phone on the morning of the second, calling to politely ask what day and time they would like me to pick up the rent from them. If I get voice mail, I leave a friendly message. If I haven't had a return call by the 3rd, I both text them and voice mail them again on the 3rd about the rent, always stating that I would hate to have to collect any late fees, so to please call me as soon as possible so I know when to pick up the rent.

Never be afraid to ask your tenants for the rent. The minute they sense you are afraid to ask, they will stop paying.

You don't have to be mean or nasty in asking for the rent. I would highly recommend that you are nice about it, calm but firm. Almost matter of fact – just like when they ask for maintenance. It's my job to provide excellent customer service with prompt maintenance, and it's the tenants' job to pay their rent. They are never offended when I ask for my rent.

Also, I never allow tenants to "mail" me the rent. First of all, I don't take any checks or money orders, so mailing cash would be foolish and risky. Secondly, it's in my lease that rent is to be picked up at the tenants address. So that's the binding law in the agreed upon contract. This also prevents disreputable tenants from telling you "the check is in the mail." And then it never arrives, as you wait and worry. No, no, no – none of that nonsense for you!

Just as in dealing with your service business temp employees, your tenants *must* do things *your way.* I view tenants as employees who pay me. They have to follow my rules and regulations as spelled out in the lease. And they have to pay me for the privilege of doing so. Of course, they are getting a nice place to live and fantastic customer service on maintenance and repairs in return. So everyone gets a great deal. Win-win!

When They Just Have To Go

No matter how hard you try to treat your tenants right (and get treated right in return), sooner or later you're going to come across someone you know just has to go! About the only time I make that determination is when a tenant isn't paying the rent. I don't care *what* the excuse is. I understand only three things when it comes to the rent. *Where's my money? I want my money. Give me my money!*

If a tenant has a history of paying late, but pays *all* late fees with a smile, then I *love* that tenant, since he's making me extra money every month. If your units are paid off, that should be fine with you as well. If they're not paid off, you'll still have that emergency reserve fund we discussed earlier. So it shouldn't be a problem for you to receive your rent money late. You make an extra $100 - $200 a month, and you *still* manage to pay your mortgage on time.

The only other reason I would evict a tenant is for conducting illegal activity at my unit. Minor infractions of the lease *can* be used to evict a tenant, but I think that's being penny wise and dollar foolish. The same with the pet issue or minor tenant damages. No big deal - let it go.

But if a tenant is creating some major damage, I would think seriously about evicting him. And if he's breaking the law, you *have* to evict him or run the risk of "endorsing" his illegal activities and possibly even losing your house to the government in the case of federal violations. I would *not* recommend evicting him yourself, however, because if all of your *i's* aren't dotted and your *t's* aren't crossed, you could be wasting valuable time and money. There are eviction services that can handle the job more efficiently and even go to court for you when necessary.

Fortunately, I haven't had to evict a tenant in over a decade, but I still have a company contact on hand in case I need it. The same company also does background checks on tenants, if necessary. I tend to do the background checks myself. I tell the tenant to bring me their last two pay check stubs to the rental interview so I can quickly verify their income. There are two reasons for this. First of all corporate human resource departments aren't always the fastest at providing information on their employees – dealing with landlords is just *not* their top priority. And I like to see the actual pay check stubs myself. Any friend can lie and *say* you work at their company. A fake paycheck stub is a lot harder to come up with!

Also, you can check online to see if their last couple of rental references are legitimate. Check with your local county assessor's office to see if the guy they say owned their last house really did. If not, and the renter lied to you, he's not going to be your best bet for a reliable tenant.

I also like to talk to the second-to-last landlord the person rented from – along with the current one. Sometimes, a current landlord will give a glowing reference on a bad tenant just to get him out of his house without having to pay for the eviction process. But the landlord *before* that one has nothing to gain by lying and will likely give you the unvarnished truth for sure!

Hopefully, after doing your landlording homework carefully, conducting your background checks diligently, and treating your tenants well, you won't *ever* have to face the eviction process - or at least not often. But it's nice to know that, if one of your tenants suddenly stops paying or engages in illegal activities, there are laws on the books to help you get him out.

Love What You Do

Whether or not you ever have to face that possibility, by this time in your life, you should have a pretty good understanding of what's involved in real-estate rentals. You should have a good idea of whether or not you love - absolutely *love* - being a landlord. I'm betting you do.

After all, what's not to love? Easy work, short hours, great returns on your investment, and a short road to success. From here on out it's only a matter of time.

You build a business, you make money. You buy a building, you make more money. You grow your business, you make more money still. You buy another building with the profits, you make more money *still*.

Where will you stop? When do you call it quits?

I'd tell you, but I haven't found that point in my life yet.

Yes, I'm "retired." I've been officially retired for over a decade. But that doesn't mean I've quit having fun. And some of the most fun I've ever had in life has been in creating more wealth.

Creating wealth from growing your service business and owning your rental properties is a very simple recipe for *your* financial success.

You've earned it. Enjoy!

CHAPTER SEVENTEEN

How to Choose and Train a Manager for Your Service Business

Ok, whether you started it from scratch or purchased a ready-made business, you are now a very seasoned and successful service business owner. And you have purchased at least one and possibly by now several rental properties, maybe even enough to retire on the rental income alone. Nice job!
Everything is clicking along like clockwork. Your rentals are bringing you a nice chunk of money each month as well as giving you great income tax breaks. Your service business is making you lots of money as well. You are saving large chunks of money each month, you are living comfortably, and you're well on your way to early retirement.

Hire a Manager or Sell Your Business?
So now you have a choice to make. Do you want to actually sell the service business that you built up to such a

nice level of profitability? Or do you want to keep it and find a manager to run it for you? All the while continuing to invest in more rental properties. Or you could also start to invest into paper assets if your rental income is now at least twice your monthly income or greater.

If you decide you want to sell the service business and just dive head first into rentals as your primary source of income, that's just fine. Everyone needs a place to live, so you will always have tenants to provide you with an income. And rentals also follow inflation – when prices go up, so do rents. If prices go down, rents may drop slightly. Either way, your purchasing power remains the same. So it's a super safe investment. Most wealthy people tend to keep the bulk of their assets in real estate and in businesses. And now you have both.

So if you decide to sell, I'll tell you how to do that in the next chapter. But if you want to hire a manager and keep both sources of income for the long haul, that's perfectly fine as well. There is never just one right way to do anything. And you can easily retire with rentals *and* a service business – as long as you hire the right manager for your service business.

Promoting From Within or Hiring an Outside Manager
I'm not big on the idea of hiring an outside manager, and there are several reasons why. First of all, I have never worked with this person before, so I have no idea about their honesty, integrity, loyalty, dependability, personality, manners, professionalism, customer service or sales abilities, or their work ethic. Next, that "outside manager" doesn't know a thing about performing the actual service, because they have never done it before.

How can someone supervise your workers if they don't even understand what is required to do the job properly? How can an outside manager correct your temporary employees or know if they just need to be replaced?   To me, these are just too many unknowns to want to deal with. Which why I always prefer to promote from within. Then you know who you are getting.

How to Select Your Manager

So I would look over all my temp employees and ask myself some questions about them. *Who is the most dependable and never ever calls in sick to work? Who always shows up on time and often is early? Who works late or weekends if needed with a happy smile and great attitude – each and every time? Who comes to me on a regular basis saying "Hey boss, I'm done with the current work, what do you want me to do now?" (Instead of just hiding and slacking off until quitting time). Who sees that something needs to be done and just does it, even if it's not part of their regular job description? Who is totally honest with me and has never lied to me about anything ever? Who cares more about my business than their fellow employees, who will come to me and let me know if one of my workers is slacking off? Who is responsible and has never made an excuse if he did happen to make a mistake? Who has the most presentable appearance – consistently clean cut, clean clothes, neat appearance – never disheveled or wrinkled? Who is the most professional, has the best manners and is always courteous to everyone? Who never cusses, even while away from work? Who has the confidence and basic grammatical skills to speak intelligently with customers at a sales presentation? Who is the most motivated to succeed and would kill for a chance to better his life by becoming my manager? And who would be grateful to me forever for that chance? And who is loyal enough that given that chance to be my manager, he would want to work for me forever? Who is always willing to do things my way, without question, and with a great attitude? Who has an attitude of gratitude?*

By asking yourself these questions about your temporary employees, you will know who is the most suitable to become your manager. And the beauty of promoting from within is that you already know that this full time temporary employee is extremely familiar with almost every aspect of your business and that he's also very good with your customers, professional, courteous, and customer service oriented.

One last benefit to promoting from within, is that if one

of your full-time temps ever calls in sick, your new manager is already trained in the service routes, and he can fill in for your sick employee for the day, without the hassle of having to train someone new for just a day.

So the only real training you would have to do is to teach them how to continue your marketing efforts, how to do sales presentations, and how to close the deal. You would also have to teach them how to handle the customer service aspects in dealing with potential and actual clients (Make a friend, Make a sale). And you would need to explain to them the system for how to handle any problems promptly and properly. And make sure they have the proper business attire for sales calls and networking events. And lastly, be able to train them on any paperwork and record keeping that is required for your business.

Once you have selected your full time temp to become your manager, and he has eagerly and gratefully accepted, then I would plan on a six month *trial* management training program. Letting your temp know it is a trial period tells him that if he doesn't work out, he goes back to the service only side of the business. A little bit of carrot and stick (carrot is the promotion, stick is the possibility of losing the promotion) will make your manager trainee try *even harder* to meet and even exceed your expectations.

During this trial period, he will be glued to your side so that you can teach him everything he needs to know in both theory and practice. The first thing you would need to do is immediately hire another temp to replace him on his service route. Then I would accompany your new manager trainee on that route and supervise him training your new temp. Since he's the one you chose to be manager, he should be an expert at doing the service.

Teaching isn't always as easy as following instructions, however, so you want to be there to make sure he doesn't drop the ball on teaching the ropes to your new temp. Just as your new manager will be training and correcting your new temp on the service route, you will be training and correcting your new manager on how to train the new temp in case he leaves out anything that you need your new temp to know.

Once that new temp is trained and ready to go off on his own, and you feel secure in the knowledge that your new manager is capable of training any future temps without your supervision, now it's time to train him on the other aspects of the management position.

Business Attire

Ask to see your new managers business attire. If it's already up to snuff, great. But it's actually unlikely he'll have any business clothes if he's been doing manual labor for you in your service business. If that's the case, take him to your local thrift shop and help him select that same business wardrobe that I recommended to you in earlier chapters. Once you have him properly outfitted and he's purchased his new (used) clothes, he'll be ready to learn the next steps.

Marketing, Sales Presentations, Deal Closings, Customer Service and Problem Solving...

Now it's time to make your manager your shadow. For about a month, just have him go with you and observe. You still do the work on your own, and have him watch, listen and learn. Encourage him to ask you questions. While you travel from appointment to appointment, ask him questions while you are in the car, to see if he understands your system. Ask him the difference between a hard sale and a soft sale? Ask him which he thinks is the right way to do it? If he guesses the wrong answer, gently correct him and explain to him *why* soft selling is so important.

Explain to him the philosophy of "Make a friend, Make a sale." Explain to him your system of taking notes on all potential and current customers and their personal information, so that he can later ask about the customer's wife Marie, his son Sam who is majoring in journalism, and the latest model airplane show that your client may have attended. Explain to him how to "close a sale" and give him examples of "closing questions." Then ask him to give *you* a sales presentation and you pretend to be the customer and ask him lots of questions.

See how he does. Give him gentle but constructive criticism to explain the proper way to do anything that he isn't doing "just quite right" yet. Repeat this exercise until he has it down pat.

Explain to your new manager why all of this is critical to the success of your business. Then ask him to explain it all back to you, so that you can see he actually understands what you are trying to convey to him. If he doesn't get it on the first try, keep explaining and keep quizzing him until he gets it.

Explain to your new manager why it's so important to solve problems in the way I explained earlier. And that that is the *only* acceptable way to solve any and all problems, *always*. Make sure he understands by asking him to explain it back to you, how to handle the problems and why it's the right way. If he can explain it back to you, he gets it. If he doesn't get it on the first try, keep drumming it into his head until he *does* get it. You can also role play a little bit, with you being the angry, screaming, unreasonable customer and seeing how he handles he situation. These aspects are so important to your business success, that if he *never* gets it, you better find yourself a new manager.

However, it's likely that if you selected your best temp employee, who fit all the criteria listed above, he should be very eager and very committed to learn your business practices in order to keep this prized position as your manager. So it shouldn't take him long to understand your business philosophies.

One other important thing to remember when training your new manager. You want him to succeed, and so therefore you want him to learn. So you want to provide him with an atmosphere that promotes learning and encourages him.

When people are faced with anger, disappointment or pressure, the ability to learn usually flies right the window. So if it takes a little bit of repetition with your new manager to get everything straight in his head, that's ok. That's why you are giving him a six month training period. Don't make him feel bad. Praise him when he gets something right. Don't get angry or show dismay when he gets something wrong. Just gently correct him. Sort of like toilet training a child or house training a puppy, you have to gently lead him along to what you want him to do.

Being a gentle trainer will garner you even more loyalty from your new manager. And the reason is because he is already nervous and wanting to impress you and not wanting to blow his one chance to go from a manual laborer making a fixed hourly wage to a manager who not only gets the prestige of his new title, he gets the chance to make even more money as he makes you more money. So be gentle, kind and diplomatic when you are training and correcting him.

Also take him to networking events, cold calling and actual sales appointments, again, so he can watch and learn. Introduce him to your potential and actual clients as your associate. That way if he bombs out as management material, you don't have to explain any further to your clients if he stops showing up with you. If he is the success you think he will be, *then and only then,* will you introduce him as your new manager.

The Next Step

So now your new manager trainee has learned to train your temporary workers, he has learned how to "dress for success" and he has spent about a month being your shadow – just watching and learning everything you do and practicing his sales presentation on you. And also practicing his handling of problem customers on you. If you are satisfied that he is ready, now I would become *his* shadow. Let him do all the marketing, cold calling, networking, customer service and any problem solving – and you just tag along and watch, listen and learn.

If overall he is doing great but flounders a little here or there, you can diplomatically step in to close the deal or correct his handling of the situation. Let him know in advance that if you step in, he is to step back, be quiet, listen and learn. Then after that meeting, in the car, explain what he was doing that was not quite right, and go over the proper way to handle a situation and why. At this point he'll basically just need some minor tweaking while you accompany him.

After about a month of this, he should be ready to

handle anything. But you still need to be sure. So for the next three months, go with him on everything, but you just watch and learn and evaluate how he is doing. If anything needs correcting, then gently correct him. But if he is completely competent at this point and growing your business as well, stick around a couple more months to make sure there are no little hiccup areas you may have overlooked, just to be extra safe. At that point, you can safely take him around to all your clients and introduce him as your new full time sales and customer service manager.

Make it clear to all your clients that your new manager is their new contact person. But also make it crystal clear that if there is *ever* a situation that your new manager doesn't handle to their satisfaction, you are still just as interested in your client's well-being as ever, and that they are always, always, *always* welcome to call you on your cell phone for immediate attention from you personally. That protects you from your new manager running your business into the ground, although that's unlikely at this point. And it also let's your new manager know that he is still constantly being watched and reported on (if necessary) by your current and future clients.

On any future new clients, I would make sure to provide your new manager with an updated version of your "Welcome letter" that explains that Joe Temp is their sales and customer service manager. However, should there *ever* be *any* situation in which they find they aren't satisfied for *any* reason, to call you, as the owner of the company, for immediate and personal attention to fix any problem. Again, this protects you from any mishaps with your new customers and your new manager. It also keeps your clients watching him for any problems, so you don't have to!

Payment and Motivation

Let's pretend that your full time temp has been paid $9 an hour from the temp agency to work for you. So you of course pay a little more than that to the temp agency so that they can pay all his workers comp and unemployment insurance, his withholding taxes, etc. and make a little profit for themselves. When you promote your temp to manager, I would call the temp agency and tell them to give him a fifty cent an hour raise, which they will happily do for you. On top of that, I would tell your new manager that for every new monthly customer he lines up for you, he will earn a bonus of 5% of that client's monthly service fee for *each and every month* that he keeps that client. And for any client he loses (for whatever the reason) while acting as your manager, you will dock his pay 5% of that client's monthly service fee for *each and every month thereafter.* In this way, you are tying his success to your success.

The more money he makes for you, the more money *he* makes as well. If he loses you money (which he is not supposed to do) then he loses money too. Fair is fair. In this way, if he lands you a whale paying $4,000 a month, his income will increase $200 a month for every month that you have that customer. If he loses that customer, he loses that $200 a month from his pay. See how nicely this works? If you win, he wins. If you lose, he loses. If he's the great manager I expect he will be, he will move heaven and earth to keep your customers – and to get new ones! And that's what you want most in your manager.

To show you the numbers, if your new manager has landed you a $4,000 a month whale, 5% of that is just $200 a month. Divide $200 by 160 hours (that's 4 work weeks, 8 hours a day, 5 days a week = 160 man hours). It works out to $1.25 more an hour that you will pay your temp. A nice reward for him and certainly a nice reward he gave you. Every new client he gets you ups his pay. And any client he loses reduces his pay. Suppose he lost you a $200 a month account. 5% of that is $10. $10 divided by 160 man hours equals 6 cents. So now you lower his pay by 6 cents an hour. It may not seem like much to you, but for an hourly employee, every nickel counts. He will want to continue to increase his pay every month, and he will have the power to do so!

And depending on your profit margins, you can change the percentage to better suit your business needs. Perhaps 10%, 15% or even 20% is a better amount to motivate your manager, while still making you a bundle. Only you can decide, based on the actual costs involved in your particular service business.

And as your new temp manager has his pay increased or decreased, you simply call the temp agency and say "Hey, Joe Temp and I have agreed his pay will be increased to $11.50 an hour now" if he's landed you some new clients. Or if he has lost a client, you call the temp agency and say "Joe Temp and I have agreed his pay will be decreased to $10.75 an hour until further notice." But likely you will have many more increases than decreases, since your new manager's success is directly tied to yours.

You'll also need to train your new temp manager on any paperwork that needs to be done. This is simple enough. Show him how, then have him do it and correct him in any areas that need correcting. The one thing I would not have your temp manager do is handle the money. Sure, he can do the invoicing, and open the business bills and write out the checks (but not sign them!) and prepare the bank deposits, and keep all the appropriate record keeping that you will show him how to do. But *only you* will be handling the bank deposits and the signing of checks for vendors as needed.

And make sure at least once a month you look over your newly updated customer list, the copies of the invoices sent, the list of who has paid and not paid, and see the bills that match the checks you are to sign for payment. That lets your temp manager know you are not totally lost in space, that there are checks and balances, and you are always watching. While we certainly expect his honesty based on past performance, you never ever want to give your employees an opportunity to steal from you. An ounce of prevention is worth way more than a pound of cure!

CHAPTER EIGHTEEN

How and When to Sell Your Service Business

After you've owned and run your service business for a while and have gotten your feet wet in landlording, there's going to come a time when you should think about selling your business.

What? Sell your sweat and toil? Sell your brainchild? Sell your *baby?*

Absolutely. It's your next step toward making a fortune and retiring early. Using the proceeds from the sale your service business will be your down payment on the next investment in your life.

But how do you know *when* to sell your business? And where do you find a buyer? And how much should you ask? After all, there's not exactly a Big Book of Businesses for Sale. *Is there?*

Always Use a Business Broker!

I sold my lingerie business to the girl who did management for me for several years. I sold her the lingerie at cost, so I basically got my $1,000 initial investment back and nothing more. I could have sold it for a much higher price if I'd gone through a business broker.

When I sold my nightclub, I tried going through a business broker, but since it was a losing proposition until I got the club running in the black, the minimum commission to pay the business broker would have been *more* than I could sell the business for. So I placed an ad in the local newspaper, and sold it for $15,000. That was probably more than it was worth at the time, but I wasn't about to complain!

With my pet sitting business, again, I should have used a business broker, but my plant business was taking off and I wanted to get rid of the pet sitting business as quickly as possible so I could focus on my plant business. So I put an ad in the local business and sold it for $1,500. Once again, I could have gotten a lot more if I had used a broker. I want *you* to benefit from *my* mistakes, so I highly recommend *always* selling your business through a broker…and here is *why*.

When I finally sold my plant business, I did use a business broker, and he did a free evaluation of it's worth. There are a few different methods that brokers use to determine the value of a business, and they all came out to around the same general amount. My business was estimated to be worth $475,000!!! Talk about a great sounding number to make off an initial investment of only $1,000 not even ten years earlier! $475,000 plus my savings combined were more than enough for me to retire comfortably. And now you know why I strongly recommend you sell your business using a business broker. I'm sure I could be worth a lot more today if I had sold my prior businesses using a broker. But that's why I'm sharing my knowledge in this book – so that you can learn – and then *earn* – from my mistakes.

I took the brokers estimate and put the business on the market immediately. A while afterwards, I was involved a serious car accident that banged me up badly – all because my seatbelt hadn't locked and the airbag hadn't deployed. I needed time to recuperate. I needed to sell my plant business *pronto* in order to be able to focus on getting well.

I was in so much pain that I didn't care *how* my business was doing, so I knew I needed to sell it quickly before I lost all my customers and any ability to sell it at all! Unfortunately, selling any business takes time – often a year or more – and that was time I didn't have.

So I calculated the bare minimum I needed in order to retire. I subtracted what I had in savings from that number. And then I sold the business for the difference, which was a huge discount from it's original evaluation price. But I needed to get rid of it fast, as I just couldn't run it properly while recuperating.

As it turned out, it was the right decision at the time. Sure, I might have been able to hang onto it while convalescing, but why run the risk? A bird in the hand, as the old saying goes.

How Much Is It Worth?

There are many ways to determine the value of a business for sales purposes. The simplest is to call a broker and ask him to do it for you. He'll use several different tried-and-true methods to accurately determine what your business is worth. And remember that any reputable business broker will do this evaluation *free of charge.* If a broker tries to charge you for the evaluation, run for the hills. That broker is not in the business of selling businesses, he's in the business of selling evaluations! Just like a reputable real estate agent will give you a free evaluation of your home's value in hopes of landing you as a client, a legitimate business broker will give you a free evaluation of the expected sales price of your business. Just like honest and reputable attorneys and CPAs will give you a free consult – they do this is in hopes of landing you as a client as well as seeing if they are the right attorney or CPA for your particular situation.

If the broker comes up on the low side of what you were expecting, feel free to ask him questions: *How did you arrive* at your figures? What method did you use? How confident are you that our figures are accurate? Once you get the answers you want, don't stop there! Have two or three other brokers give you *their* best estimates as to what your business is worth. Don't tell any of the brokers what the others have come up with, and never give a broker a minimum price that you would be willing to accept. If you tell a broker that you'd be happy settling for $200,000 and he knows that your business is worth twice that amount, an unscrupulous broker might low-ball you on the price in order to make a fast sale and get a quick commission.

Deciding When to Sell

So now you have a pretty good idea of the market value of your business. But how do you know when is the best time to sell? Here's how I handle that question.

1. **When your rentals are paying your way.** *Never sell your service business until your rental units are capable of providing you with twice as much income as your total monthly living expenses.* And even then, remember that the longer you maintain two sources of income (your service business and your rentals), the faster your savings will accumulate, the more rental units you can purchase, and the sooner you'll be able to retire and be financially free!

2. **When the competition is too great.** It's also a good idea to consider selling when you begin facing increased competition in your service area. A greater number of service businesses similar to yours means fewer customers to go around; fewer clients to sign up; fewer profits to share. In such a case, it's wise to sell out *before* the other businesses steal all your clients from you. If you have been diligently following my plan, you should have enough rentals to retire on, and if not, the sale of your business should generate enough money to buy enough rentals

to retire on. So take the bird in the hand!

3. **When you are burned out.** It could be that you are like me, and after a few years of making lots of money and then buying up your real estate, you just get bored, burned out or are ready to make a change. You know you have enough to retire on with your real estate, and you are just ready to enjoy the good life!

4. **When you have a medical issue.** It could be that you have a debilitating car accident (like me), cancer or some other horrible disease (like my ex-husband) and you just need to concentrate on your health and recuperation. As long as you have enough rentals or you'll have enough money to buy enough rentals to retire on after the sale, I say go for it!

From my own standpoint, I've never worked so little and made so much money as I have as a landlord. *Ever!*

Finding a Buyer for Your Business
A lot of people new to self-employment are surprised to find that there are buyers for virtually every business imaginable. My business broker did the work of advertising for me. Brokers have a set-up similar to that of real estate agents – a listing service for businesses, so to speak.

The broker I used in Las Vegas when I sold my plant business charged a percentage of the sales price, just as realtors do when selling a house. In fact, a broker can even tell you how profitable your business needs to be in order to sell it for "X" number of dollars. Then, you'll know how much bigger you'll need to make your business profits before reaching your goal and listing your business for sale.

Things to Watch Out For
Of course, as with anything, there are potential pitfalls you'll want to avoid when selling a business.

For starters, make sure you understand the terms of the sale. There should be no "minimum" commission – the broker gets *only* a percentage of the sales price. In that way, he's motivated to get you the highest possible price, since more money to you means more money for him.

Also, a broker will have a legal contract for you to sign. Always read over your business contracts yourself – *all* of them – to make sure you understand what you are signing. But before signing anything, notate any questions you have so that you can ask both your broker and your lawyer about them. Even after you have reviewed the contracts yourself, it's always a good idea to have your attorney look over the entire contract, to look for any red flags you might have missed.

Also, I suggest you interview a few different brokers to see who you feel most comfortable with. Good rapport as well as expertise is important in all business relationships. You'll want to find a broker you enjoy working with.

See if all the brokers you interview come up with similar prices for your business. Ask them what they base their evaluations on so that you understand where they are coming from. If they all come up in the same ballpark range, that shows they all know what they are doing. But if one comes up with a super low or a super high number, I would be skeptical of that broker. I'd ask *why* there's such a difference in price when three other brokers gave you a lower or higher amount, for example.

I suggest you also ask for at least three verifiable references that you can contact to see what type of experience they had with the broker. Did they complete a successful sale of their businesses? Did they get close to the price the broker set in the beginning? Would they use that broker again? What were the names of their businesses and who did they sell them to? Then check their answers with the Secretary of State and the buyers of those businesses to see if those sales actually went through.

Also, ask the broker what type of connections he has with the SBA (Small Business Association), in case your buyer needs to get an SBA loan. If the broker can walk the buyer through this process or has connections in the SBA, all the better. That makes it that much easier to get the sale done.

And speaking of the SBA, don't shy away from dealing with them. Think of them as a mortgage lender for a house sale. It takes a little time, but you'll get your money eventually, once your buyer gets his loan approved. One thing I would *not* do is to take a note for your business (carry the paper). Just as with a house sale, you want to get your money and run. If you have agreed to finance a note and accept monthly payments from the buyer, instead of getting the full purchase price in cash up front, if your buyer runs your business into the ground, you and your future are doomed. You will never get your money out of the buyer. And you can't repossess your business because now it's worthless. And all the hard work you spent building a successful, wonderful business will be wasted. Always, always, *always* get the cash in hand. Once the deal is completed, you can put that business venture out of your mind and concentrate on more important things...like your early retirement!

Setting Your Asking Price

Once you've found the business broker of your dreams and settled on a fair value for your business, you'll need to determine an asking price. Remember that the asking price is not the same as the actual value of your business. If your business is valued at $500,000, you do *not* want to go into negotiations asking $500,000, or you're absolutely *guaranteed* to come up short. So what asking price do you start out with? And how do you determine one that's realistic and not ridiculous?

Here's a way for you to set an asking price that should land you very close to the price you actually desire. Let's say you went to three different business brokers. Add all three estimates together and divide by three. This is the average estimate, and likely the most realistic price for your business. For example, if three different brokers gave me estimates of $470,000, $479,000 and $482,000 (all in the same range), the average of those three estimates would be $477,000, and that is the price I would want to end up with. So I would list my property at 10 – 15 percent *above* that average price, or from $524,700 to $548,550, so there is room to negotiate. I could then come down quite a bit on my asking price and know I'm *still* getting top dollar.

The advantage to this method of selling is that everyone walks away feeling good. Remember that buyers like to feel as if they have "won" a negotiation or gotten a really great deal. If you start your negotiations at a higher figure than you are willing to accept, you can negotiate down and allow the buyer to purchase for less than the original asking price. The result – the buyer feels as if he has *won* something, and you're happy because you got the price that you actually wanted from the start. Win-win.

Of course, there aren't always that many buyers ready to purchase a business, since probably 90 percent of all human beings are employees rather than employers. That means you're not likely to have a *huge* number of buyers clamoring to purchase your business. So, treat each offer with serious consideration, since it might be your only offer for *months*.

In the 1-1/2 years during which my plant business was for sale, I received only two or three offers *total*. During that time period, I managed to save up another year-and-a-half's worth of income. So after my car accident, I was able to sell the business quickly at a huge discount and still make out like a bandit.

My major concern had been ending up with the total figure I needed for my early retirement. I figured out how much I'd have between my savings and the proceeds from the sale of the business and how much rental income that would generate for me. Then I compared the monthly rental income I would have versus how much I need to live on each month. My monthly rental income would be lots more than twice my monthly living expenses. Once I saw that the numbers worked, I signed on the dotted line and signed up for my early retirement!

Then I purchased as many more rental units as I could and my income continued to go up, up, *up!*

Just as you're going to do.

Are *you* ready to begin exploring the very heart of your early retirement program? Are you ready to take the next leap?

CHAPTER NINETEEN

Your Five *Easy* Steps to Wealth and Early Retirement

As your wealth continues to grow, be careful not to fall into the trap of thinking you're instantly "rich" and can go out and buy anything you want. Remember that what you want most is an early retirement. Not a fancy car, not a fancy house, not a super-fancy cruise around the world. Treat yourself to little rewards now and again as a means of renewing your desire to succeed. Life has to have a little fun in it! But resist the bigger temptations.

Live Low, Save High!
Keep in mind that, even as your income grows, you'll want to keep your monthly expenses low. In that way, you'll continue building your investment nest egg so that you can continue to buy more rental houses. Don't spend every nickel you earn – that's a recipe for homelessness if even the smallest financial emergency arises. Instead, *always live below your*

means, so that you'll always be saving more than you're spending and outpacing inflation.

When I was really poor, I always tried to live on half of what I earned. In that way, I always had a built-in safety net and my savings continued to grow. I have never forgotten how that $1,500 I had squirreled away in the bank saved my life when mom tossed me out of the house. Except for those savings, I would have been in dire straits. Remember - *live low, save high!*

By this point in your program, you should have acquired from five or six or more rental units, and everything should be running like clockwork. You continued growing your service business until you had two times more money coming in than going out, at which time you sold your business for more investment income. If not, it may be time to think about doing so now.

Of course, you may also have decided to keep your service business running while hiring a manager to oversee it. Either way works well. Just remember to keep buying rental houses until you're clearing two times your cost of living. In that way, you'll be saving a *ton* of money and staying *well* ahead of inflation. That means you'll be on safe financial ground and be set for the rest of your life.

Remember - money isn't everything. But it can fix *almost* any problem that arises.

Once you have reached the number of rental units required to provide you with twice your monthly expenses, you can think about whether or not you want to continue acquiring more rentals or place your excess income in another investment. In that case, I would suggest you consider investing in laddered, investment grade, tax-free municipal bonds. They're not paying much in interest right now, but they do save you on taxes, and money not paid in on taxes is money that's made! Or you can put your excess earnings into FDIC insured laddered CDs (Certificates of Deposit). Again, they aren't paying much in interest right now either, but your money is safe and sound in both investments.

CDs generally pay slightly higher interest rates than tax

free munis, but that interest is taxable, so it depends on your tax bracket to decide which is the better investment. Your CPA can advise you here. The "laddering" of both insured tax free municipal bonds or of FDIC insured CDs insures that one investment is always coming due on at regular intervals, which comes in handy if you have a sudden need for a large amount of cash. You can ladder these investments to make sure that some investment is *always* coming due either monthly, quarterly, every six months, or once a year. Whatever works for you.

Do not buy more CDs at any one bank than are covered by FDIC insurance. And don't keep any more money in any one bank's accounts than is covered by the FDIC. That insurance amount is currently $250,000. Be sure you keep current on the laws for your own protection. Generally speaking, I think it's a wise practice to spread your income around to more than one bank and more than one municipal bond.

A word of advice on CDs and tax-free municipal bonds. While some investors talk them down because they're presently paying low interest rates, I like them. They're safe, and their lower rates mean they can only go in one direction: Up! By the time you have your service business running on auto pilot and have bought all the rental units you need and have possibly sold your business, the economy will likely be in much better shape than it was in 2011. Besides, even a 5 - 6% return on your extra investment money isn't bad for doing nothing!

Maintain Control of Your Finances

Part of your successful wealth-building program involves maintaining control of all aspects of your life that can affect your finances, for good or bad. That includes your credit score. Keep it as high as possible. It will help you to get lower interest rates on mortgage loans, lower car insurance rates, better credit-card rates, and possibly even a higher return on your bank accounts. Also, you never can predict when a great house deal is going to come along, and you want to be prepared to jump on it - providing you have the down payment, it meets your criteria for investment properties, and the numbers work. A high credit rating may be just what you need to make that purchase a reality.

Diversification and Investments to Avoid

Another way to maintain control over your finances is to diversify your investments. Besides business ownership, rental units, FDIC insured CDs, and insured tax-free municipal bonds, you may want to buy into some other investments for diversification. I suggest you continue investing in CDs and tax-free munis, but you might also want to consider the risks and possible benefits of other investments. You could also talk to a financial advisor, but since I don't trust them personally, I can't suggest that action to you.

Investment counselors and financial advisors are basically salesmen, and as such they sometimes have their own best interests at heart instead of yours. And you won't usually know if they are untrustworthy until it's too late and all your money is gone. Of course there are plenty of honest ones out there, but I have heard too many horror stories from friends that were sold bad investments just because the financial advisor made a giant commission off them.

Two examples of high commission investments that are often inappropriate for the investor are "whole or universal life insurance policies" and "annuities." In certain circumstances, an annuity *may* be very appropriate for you. But unfortunately annuities are sold to far too many people for whom it's an inappropriate investment, all so that an unscrupulous financial planner can make a super high commission – which is why they try to push them onto everyone, appropriate or not. I would ask your CPA his opinion here, as he can give an objective opinion regarding your particular circumstances, before you buy any type of annuity. On whole life insurance policies, I can't think of single instance where that is an appropriate investment for *anyone.* If you need life insurance, stick with a term life insurance policy instead.

The easiest and safest way to diversify your investment portfolio is to invest for the long term in indexed mutual funds.

They allow you to own a small piece of the entire world market - and you can do that without using a financial advisor or paying any commissions. Buy one fund for the entire U.S. Stock Market, one fund for the entire International Market, one fund for Precious Metals as a hedge against a devalued U.S. dollar, and a Dividend Equity fund (which is made up of dividend paying stocks).

You can dollar cost-average into those each month. That means you buy a set dollar amount of the investment each month. If you have a total of $1,200 to invest in a certain mutual fund, you would divide that cost by 12 monthly purchases spread out over a year and buy $100 worth of that fund each month. In that way, there's less risk of your buying $1,200 worth of the fund on the one day of the year it happens to hit an all-time high! In fact, by buying a set dollar amount each month, you're almost certain to get a better deal than if you buy all the shares at once.

And remember that we're talking about how to invest *after* you've secured your early retirement rental income of twice your monthly expenditures. And before putting your funds into *any* uninsured investment to *do due diligence.* Ask around, get advice, run the numbers, read the prospectus, and never invest any money in paper assets *that you can't afford to lose.* You may get to the point where you have more income than time and decide to sink some of your money into a high-risk investment. Still, I suggest you keep *most* of your wealth in rental houses and insured investments - just to be safe.

And to give you a further peak into my financial life – I have approximately 74% of my total net worth invested in real estate. I have approximately 24% of my total net worth in cash (FDIC insured CDs, money market bank account and tax-free munis). I have approximately 2% of my total net worth in stocks, bonds, precious metals and mutual funds, which include shares of the following: a total US Stock Market Index Fund, a Broad International Index Fund, a Tax-Free Municipal Bond Fund, a Gold & Precious Metals Fund, a Dividend Equity Fund and some Silver and Gold. This 2% is all money I can easily afford to lose. But because I have selected carefully, I not only do not expect to lose this money, I expect to continue to invest small amounts in these investments each month and get quite a healthy return over the next 20 years. After all, at only 48 years old, I still have time on my side as far as long-term investing in the stock market goes.

Now, just because you have accumulated a certain amount of wealth and a nice relaxing leisurely lifestyle, that doesn't mean it's time to get lazy when it comes to investing. *Always* do your homework, investigate and do your due diligence before investing. There will be time enough to relax very soon. You're almost there, but not quite. Once you've finished acquiring rental property and have either sold your service business or hired someone else to manage it for you, *then* you can get very leisurely. And you'll have earned it!

Don't be surprised, though, if you find yourself looking for new challenges before a few months of lolling around aimlessly have passed. After all, it's one thing to "retire" and never work another day in your life when you're 75 and in poor health. It's something else totally to retire at the age of 38 and in the prime of your life.

So never close the door to new opportunities. My own leisurely life includes sleeping every day until I feel like getting up - no alarm clock for me! After that, I feed the kitties, turtles and fish, brush my teeth, and get reasonably presentable for the day. I don't want to scare off the mailman! Then I check my email and see if any tenants have an issue that needs attention. If a tenant does need attention, then I spend from 5 - 10 minutes making telephone calls to arrange for those items to be done. Then I cook a veggie omelet breakfast and read the paper until noon.

After that, I run whatever errands I have or plan some fun project. I enjoy a leisurely lunch whenever I feel like it. Possibly visit friends, or go shopping, or do some charity work, and then later work out in my gym. As evening rolls around, I get ready to go dancing or bowling or to a comedy show, or I simply stay in, watch a good tv show, and cuddle with my cats.

My point is that I do whatever makes me happy. I like to be leisurely, but busy, with activities that interest me, and always at *my* pace. Occasionally I curl up with my kitty and we take a nap in the middle of the day - so wonderfully decadent! Other times I stay up all night and watch DVDs. Whatever my mood, I give in to it. It's a really delightful way to live.

Did you ever wish you could come back in your next life as someone's pampered pet? That's me - just lounging around all day, napping when I want, playing with my projects when I want, eating when I want, being social when I want. I answer to no one, and you can't be any freer than that!

K.I.S.S. and Tell

I do feel I have some obligations in life, however. Do you remember the acronym, KISS? I've changed it a little for my purposes - Keep It Successfully Simple! That's always one of my main goals. To keep my life simple. To keep my financial wealth program simple. To keep everything I do and everything I tell others how to do as simple as possible so that they learn my systems easily and they can make their lives successfully simple as well.

If you follow my five-point plan for making your own fortune and retiring early - you'll find yourself anxious to pass along your good fortune to your friends and family. My one request of you is to *do it*. Please *do* KISS and tell! The more people we can educate, the more people we can equip to make it on their own as income-generating, job creating, self-employed business people, the better everyone's lives will be.

I Have a Dream!

How wonderful would it be for everyone who is physically able to work to read my book and then be equipped with the knowledge and training to be able get off of welfare and unemployment lines, regain their dignity and need no more government handouts?

How wonderful would that be for the taxpayers?

How even more wonderful for the government officials

who were smart enough to promote my simple five-point wealth building plan?

Those government officials would become *true heroes* of our nation – saving the current tax payers *billions* of dollars and helping to balance the federal budget! And they wouldn't be kicking anyone off the entitlement programs in the meantime while people are learning. They could make my book required reading for all of the people currently on welfare, food stamps, Medicaid, Section 8 housing, and unemployment.

This book could change the lives of everyone who read it. It could change our entire nation – and all for the better!

That is my dream. I hope you *and* our politicians will help make it come true!

Follow five simple points of my wealth-growing program, going back to review this book from time to time to make sure your own five-point program is still on-track, and you'll be thanking me all the way to the bank – or the country club!

Poverty Sucks!
How to Become a Self-Made Millionaire
Five-Point Plan Review

1. Build a service business you love and grow it until it's netting you twice your monthly expenses, then save up a six month emergency fund.

2. Save up a down payment and reserve fund, then buy your first rental house.

3. Expand into more rental properties until you're earning twice your monthly expenses.

4. Either sell your service business or hire a manager to run it for you.

5. Become a pampered lazy cat and do whatever your heart desires.

Ready to join the club? Ready to cash in on all that income just waiting for you to come along and claim it? Ready to start receiving your own "money in the mail"?

The time is now. Today. This very minute.

Until then, remember one last important thought that has sustained and inspired me over the years: I never want my tombstone to say "I wish I'd worked *more!*"

To learn more about our e-business consulting:

Visit our website at:
www.AimeeElizabeth.net

CPSIA information can be obtained at www.ICGtesting.com
Printed in the USA
LVOW060441261112
308773LV00001B/222/P